LEARN FROM ME

An exposition of the Sermon on the Mount

Fr Con Buckley

Learn from Me: An exposition of the Sermon by Fr Con Buckley

ISBN 978-1-955136-00-6 (Paperback)
ISBN 978-1-955136-01-3 (Hardback)

This book is written to provide information and motivation to readers. Its purpose is not to render any type of psychological, legal, or professional advice of any kind. The content is the sole opinion and expression of the author, and not necessarily that of the publisher.

Copyright © 2021 by Fr Con Buckley

All rights reserved. No part of this book may be reproduced, transmitted, or distributed in any form by any means, including, but not limited to, recording, photocopying, or taking screenshots of parts of the book, without prior written permission from the author or the publisher. Brief quotations for noncommercial purposes, such as book reviews, permitted by Fair Use of the U.S. Copyright Law, are allowed without written permissions, as long as such quotations do not cause damage to the book's commercial value. For permissions, write to the publisher, whose address is stated below.

Printed in the United States of America.

New Leaf Media, LLC
175 S. 3rd Street, Suite 200
Columbus, OH 43215
www.thenewleafmedia.com

"Learn from me for I am meek and humble of heart, and you will find rest for your souls" (Mt.11:29-30).

This book is dedicated to my brother Jerry
who passed away recently

Table of Contents

Foreword xi

Chapter 1: Introduction 1
Chapter 2: The Wisdom Structure of the Sermon 7
Chapter 3: The First Beatitude, Blessed are the
               Poor in Spirit 15
Chapter 4: The First Beatitude's relevance for Today 23
Chapter 5: Blessed are the meek (gentle), they
               shall have the earth for their heritage 32
Chapter 6: The Relevance of the Second Beatitude 36
Chapter 7: Happy are those who Mourn for they
               shall be Comforted 40
Chapter 8: The Relevance of the Third Beatitude
               for Today 44
Chapter 9: Blessed are those who Hunger and
               Thirst for what is Right for they shall
               be Satisfied 48
Chapter 10: The relevance of the Fourth
                Beatitude for today 52

Chapter 11:	Blessed are the merciful	56
Chapter 12:	The Relevance of Mercy for our Age	62
Chapter 13:	Blessed are the Pure in Heart	67
Chapter 14:	The Relevance of this Beatitude for every Culture and Age	71
Chapter 15:	Blessed are the Peacemakers for they shall be called Children of God	76
Chapter 16:	The Universality of Christ's Peace Vision	81
Chapter 17:	Blessed are those who are persecuted for the sake of right; their's is the Kingdom of heaven	89
Chapter 18:	The 4 Motivational Bases	96
Chapter 19:	The Antitheses	108
Chapter 20:	The Second Antithesis: Healthy Sexual Attitudes and Relations	116
Chapter 21:	The third antithesis: enduring love and marriage fidelity as images of God's faithful love	124
Chapter 22:	The Fourth Antithesis and the Sacrament of Marriage	130
Chapter 23:	The Fifth Antithesis: honoring one's Word	140
Chapter 24:	The Sixth Antithesis: Passive Resistance	145
Chapter 25:	The Seventh Antithesis: Loving One's Enemies	151
Chapter 26:	Spiritual bases and reasons for the way of the Beatitudes	157

Chapter 27: The Our Father, the perfect prayer of the Kingdom 163

Chapter 28: Thy will be done On Earth as it is in Heaven 168

Chapter 29: The 12 Spiritual Paths 177

Chapter 30: (7)   Respecting Sacred Things 194

Chapter 31: Being a True Disciple 203

Chapter 32: Is the Sermon Excessive Idealism? 207

Chapter 33: Conclusion 213

Select Bibliography 221

FOREWORD

This study is a follow on book from my series of sermons for every Sunday of the year on the internet which are popular and were published under the title **Wheels of Light** *(see frconbuckleyssundaysermons)*. I was surprised when a young person said to me recently "this is a time of opportunity for the church". Scholarly-cum-popular commentaries on key aspects of the faith are one way of seizing the moment. We need reminders of how relevant and urgent the faith is for the times. What better way to do so than an exposition of **The Sermon on the Mount,** a seminal guide for Christian life and a sure path to peace and integrity for a perennially troubled humanity.

A new understanding of this should re-invigorate Christian and general intellectual and spiritual life, and spark a resurgence of joyful commitment to faith among the great and the good today, as earlier in our era it inspired giants from Tolstoy to Gandhi to John Paul 11. For given at the beginning of Christ's public ministry it's his heart laid bare in a divine program for humanity's happiness here and hereafter. Sadly the churches haven't always stressed its seminal importance as the happy way for humanity here and hereafter. I hope this book will help in some initial way to redress that imbalance.

For the Sermon is Christ's magnum opus, a blueprint for the world's perfective transformation. It outlines the way for each person to achieve inner peace and radiate it to others for a heaven on earth. Its beatitudes, antitheses and spiritual guidelines chart humankind's way to happiness here and salvation in the after life, as well as the way to reach these goals in a grace-filled Messianic church instituted to live and spread its gospel values.

Exploring this great project, I became ever more eager for the Sermon's better appreciation and implementation; I see it as the key to church renewal now and the eventual unity of all the churches. I hope it will similarly affect my readers for here we see the heart of Christ our Savior in love giving us the way to a healthy society and world, and a certain way to heal the brokenness of our and all times.

I thank all who helped me get this labor of love off the ground: my bishop who gave me time off parish work, my fellow priests in the diocese, Dan and Mairead who edited and commended the book, my ever supportive and encouraging family, and especially Pat Culhane and Noel Murphy to whom I owe so much.

CHAPTER 1

▼

Introduction

In 1993, John Paul 11, in **Veritatis Splendor**, restated the fundamentals of church moral teaching:

> That God has communicated the same moral requirements both as natural law, by giving human persons understanding of what is right and wrong, and as revealed truth. Since grace perfects human nature, Christian morality, while going beyond natural law, always includes it" (Grisez.36).

Anyone reflecting on the **Sermon on the Mount** must see that it is all that, and more. Jewish Scholars see it as refining the Old Testament and radicalizing the demands of the Old Covenant. Protestant scholars see it as over-idealistic, driving us to despair at its achievement. This study's shows that it "demonstrates that the Kingdom is here and that those who turn towards it will receive power to live its demands" (Fuellenbach 121).

I go further and say that it is accessible, eminently doable and that it has been lived by the best and happiest people of our age. For it's what morally ought to be, and that's what all good men and women want at heart. Sure, it's idealistic but Christ's risen presence with us until the end of time and the overflowing grace he provides makes it perfectly possible. For it is a redemptive code, not a lowest-common-denominator cop out. While having merits as far as they go, any secular moral or purely practical ethical codes can seem woefully limited when set against Christ's great blueprint for perfection which offers immense transcendent challenges and immense rewards for the soul. Yet one can argue that the Sermon is really just what all aspire to deep down; it epitomizes the universal quest for what's right and true, for humanity's fullest lived life, happiness and integrity in every way.

It's one thing to know what's right and another thing to want to and be able to do what's right. From a Christian perspective, humanity needs extra grace to do the supreme good outlined for us by God, given human weakness and imperfection. Christians have the immense advantage of the grace of the risen Lord and the church to guide them in that enabling process. For though the Spirit is accessible to all and all are saved in Christ and potentially all can attain to the truth through reason, because of man's fallen nature special helps and guidance are needed to attain to the Sermon's high level of truth and integral living.

The Christian aspect of man's ability to live the ideals of the Sermon is in what Harrington describes as "the more". More is asked of, and more is possible, within a graced Messianic community. For man cannot save himself; he needs to be saved. That is why Christ had to come, to restore humanity to its highest dignity and integrity (looking at the genocides and wars of our era, who can say man doesn't need to be redeemed). That is also why, after he was raised up,

Christ set up his church as a conduit of vital saving grace, intimate communion with God, scriptural guidance and sacramental enabling.

Thereby even the humblest Christian can be the light of the world. The Sermon provides the gospel guidance needed to see, interiorize and do the highest good more easily. So, though its high standards have been intuited and can be lived universally and non-Christian saints such as Gandhi have lived some of its key aspects, at a general level this is more difficult and the results more partial.

For the Sermon also provides a powerful spirituality to pull the cart of its ideals. The paths to deep spirituality available within the people of God enable its members to gain the inner dispositions and motivation to live the Sermon; that is why the church has produced saints in every age from St. Francis to St. John Paul 11. All seek more than mediocre living. The Sermon charts a communal righteousness made possible within a Kingdom of God church come to earth in Christ.

But it's not a moral code of arid righteousness such as the Pharisees practiced. It's a way to total human freedom in the Spirit. It charts what will unfailingly make us happy and enable us to make others happy. As such it's both eminently reasonable and more than reason; it includes the entirety of human experience; imagination, feeling, creativity, insight and love. And it adds divine wisdom, way above man's efforts to find a purely secular basis for morality: in the modern context we might cite consequentialism, proportionalism etc. in the latter regard. As John Paul 11 notes, the Sermon is the splendor of a divine ethic come to earth in Christ.

But even on a secular level, it provides the supreme objective criteria without which no moral center holds. Way beyond civic law's minimum requirements for social order, like the **Nuremberg Trials** it appeals to basic givens of civilized human behavior. It is humanity's dreams come true, a charter for joyous living, beyond all "thou shalt not" strictures or narrow arid laws (Mt 5:18).

As such it's a prophetic rather than a law-based morality. It fulfills every jot and tittle of the old law, but in the spirit. The apostles knew this in abandoning the more oppressive minute strictures of the Mosaic code. Like St. Paul does, the Sermon preaches a Christ gloriously beyond all oppressive aspects of the older law (JBC 641).

The Sermon, therefore, as John Paul 11 says, is "the Magna Carta of Gospel morality", replacing the commandments "by interiorizing their demands and bringing out their fullest meaning" (26). We are not people of law but the Spirit sent by Christ to energize his church forever. The Old Law is not false it just lacks the full prophetic Messianic dimension. That's why Christ stresses that his new way fulfills both the law and "the prophets". One wonders why traditional church manuals stressed the Ten Commandments as *the* bases for Christian morality, when Christ radically revises and completes them (e.g. "it was said to you in the past but I say to you."). Stress on the Commandments alone does not even reflect Old Testament Law; it was extended and revised in the psalms and writings of the prophets. The **Catechism of the Catholic Church** says the old law is but a first stage of divine law, a "preparation for the Gospel" (1962-64). It adds:

Finally, the Law is completed by the teaching of the sapiential books and the prophets which sets its course towards the New Covenant and the Kingdom of heaven. The New Law or the Law of the Gospel is the perfection here on earth of the divine law, natural and revealed. It is the work of Christ and is expressed particularly in the Sermon on the Mount. (1964-65)

That is, as well as the old law interiorized and refined, the Sermon is the just man of the psalms and the suffering servant of the Prophets, the Messianic Kingdom the latter predicted come into being, a kingdom and covenant that includes but goes way beyond the old Mosaic one. Its heaven on earth, humanity and divinity made one in a community that's mainly embodied now in the new Covenant people, the church, for the Beatitudes are collectives; the "poor", "the merciful", "the peacemakers" etc. They represent the values of a visible Messianic church and in its invisible dimensions, the church of all good people who do what's right and true by the lights they also receive from God. As Vatican 11 says, the church's role is "to announce and extend these Kingdom values for universal happiness" (17).

Much has been achieved of that task. We may think we live in a secular society but in fact its best aspects, what remains that are Christian of modern culture, reflects the Sermon: stress on freedom, human rights, equality, fraternity, pursuit of happiness, world peace, justice, nurture of the earth etc. So much that's good in the world echoes Christ's Sermon, though many may not advert to the fact.

But there's also much yet to be achieved, for divine wisdom, usually expressed in literary form, is never fully exhausted. Literary works are always holistic, but scriptural literature charts a deeper vision of human experience. The Sermon stretches our horizons, yet its basic principle is simple, purity within. It shows the human heart dispositions needed for heaven on earth. This Kingdom within is set against the external righteousness of religious authorities of Jesus's day: "unless your righteousness exceeds that of the scribes and the Pharisees you will not enter the Kingdom of Heaven" (Mt 5: 20).

To make reflection on the Sermon more adequate, I use modern tools of structuralist poetics which are increasingly becoming, with reader theories, a new and fertile way of opening up the scriptures. I treat the Sermon as an organic structure of infinite connectivity.

Yet this is a study for everyone. It is a reflective reading that opens up for all people this perfect guide to a happy life. I provide charts for general use and treat the work as a great symphony with ever-expanding variations on a sublime theme. The structure of this reading of the Sermon is as follows: (1) a commentary on each part of the Sermon with scholarly input and illustrative charts; (2) instances of its universal applicability, with reference to the culture of today - modern stories, books, films, popular songs; and (3) Its relation to Jesus's life, for as John Paul 11 says, the Sermon is Christ. It is his living heart laid bare before us. The key gospel phrase that sums up the Sermon, in my view is: "learn from me, for I am meek and humble in heart, and you will find rest for your souls".

CHAPTER 2

▼

The Wisdom Structure of the Sermon

Because Christ's heart of love has its logic too, there is a clear structure to the Sermon. Theologians vary in laying out this structure. There a shorter version in Luke and a longer one in Matthew so let me begin by charting the Sermon's structure in Matthew, which is the text I discuss:

Chart 1

The Plan of the Sermon

(1) The Eight Beatitudes with their apt varied blessings

The Beatitude	The Blessing
Happy the poor	Their's is the Kingdom of Heaven
Happy the gentle	They shall inherit the earth
Those who mourn	They shall be comforted

Those who hunger	They shall be satisfied
The merciful	They shall have mercy shown them
The pure in heart	They shall see God
The peacemakers..	They will be called children of God
Those persecuted for doing right	Their's is the Kingdom of Heaven
Persecuted on Christ's account	They will be great in Heaven

(2)   The Motivational Basis for Living the Beatitudes

To be the Salt of the Earth
To be the Light of the world
To Fulfill the Old Divine Law
To build Christ's new Kingdom

(3)   The "More" of the Messianic Kingdom Way, six antitheses:

"Unless your righteousness exceeds that of the scribes and Pharisees you will not enter the kingdom of heaven".

A. Thou shalt not kill.but I say to you..
B. You must not commit adultery. but I say to you..
C. Anyone who divorces his wife must give her a writ.. but I say..
D. You must not break your oath...but I say to you...
E. An eye for an eye and a tooth for a tooth..but I say..
F. Love your neighbor but hate your enemy..but I say..

(4) Three Vital Spiritual Bases for Kingdom Morality

(A) Authentic charity for God in the form of the poor, almsgiving
(B) Authentic prayer, intimate communion with God
(C) The Our Father as the summary prayer of the Kingdom

(5) 12 Spiritual Paths towards the goal of Kingdom Morality

Practicing Authentic Fasting
Building Treasure in Heaven by good works
Visionary integrity
Putting God above money
Trusting in providence
Not judging harshly
Respecting sacred goods
Believing prayer
The Golden Rule
The Narrow way
True Prophecy
Being a true Disciple of Christ

To sum up, the Beatitudes are the Sermon prologue and deal with the interior attitudes we need to be Kingdom people. Their structure is threefold, the blessing, the virtue, and the promise. The Blessing says those who practice the beatitude are happy, part of the Kingdom or ready for its reception. The virtue lists the key Kingdom attitudes: peace, mercy etc. The promise shows the rewards each virtue brings for this world and the next.

The motivational bases provide the reasons for living the beatitudes: to be the salt of the earth, the light of the world, to fulfill the Old Law and build the Messianic Kingdom for universal happiness in the final reign of God and his Christ.

The antitheses outline this new morality in more detail. They are Prophetic rewritings of the Decalogue, mainly the final seven social commandments. They give the "more" of the Kingdom, a more challenging program for Christ's new redeemed humanity.

The spiritual bases, coming at the heart of the Sermon, strip down the old law to the basics of love of God and neighbor. Love of God is shown as filial affection, right prayer, and worship summed up in the Our Father. Love of neighbor is shown as right-focused charity. As in the Gospel, the love we will be judged on is practical love of others in action: "I was hungry and you gave me to eat etc." Then at the heart of the Sermon comes its complete summary prayer, the Our Father. It is the central crescendo as it were of the Sermon symphony.

Scholars often see the 12 final exhortations as added pious practices. I see them as key spiritual activities for achieving the Way of life Christ outlines: authentic prayer, fasting, giving of alms, staying free from worldly greed, trusting in God through every trial etc. Their vital links with the beatitudes I chart as follows, related beatitudes and antitheses in parenthesis:

LEARN FROM ME: AN EXPOSITION OF THE SERMON

Chart 2

Authentic fasting and prayer (purity of heart, see God)
Building treasure in heaven (poor in spirit, gain the kingdom) Visionary integrity (purity of heart, see God)
Serving God rather than money (poor in spirit, gain the kingdom) Trusting in Providence (meek in spirit, gain the earth)
Not judging anyone (merciful, gaining God's final mercy) The golden rule (peacemakers, children of God) The narrow way (those who mourn, shall be comforted) True prophecy (thirsting for what is right, shall be satisfied)
Being a true disciple (practicing all the beatitudes, antitheses and paths)

The final crescendo of the whole symphony is the theme of true discipleship. Ultimately, the Sermon is a structure of inner righteousness leading to prophetic discipleship of Christ.

All in all the whole structure has a deep literary logic, like that of a great epic poem. The themes interrelate and reinforce each other in a cyclic dynamic. A great teacher, Christ reinforces the message in different ways, using varied devices. The main devices used are: significant balanced contradictions or antitheses; exaggerated paradoxes or oxymorons; metonymic associations that build to a complex crescendo e.g. the poor in spirit, the mourners, the merciful, the peacemakers to represent key followers of the new Kingdom (as we would say the White House to represent the American presidency); hyperbole, as in the exaggerated plucking out of one's eye if gives scandal; rich metaphoric antithetical patterns, e.g. the Kingdom metaphorically equated with entering in at the narrow gate as against the opposite way of the world metaphorically equated with entering in at the broad gate.

Rhetorical devices relate the Sermon to people's experience for this is a speech addressed to a crowd representing both disciples and humanity. Its discourse teaches us in the attractive literary way of scriptures worldwide. It's the all-wise discourse of Christ, God's teacher of his human children. My charts should make these methods and teachings clearer for teachers.

But the structure also puts flesh on the bones of Old Testament morality. Older wisdom and worship works form a series of associations in the background, e.g. the psalms and prophets. Psalm 112 virtually summarizes the whole of the beatitudes, the antitheses, the paths, and indeed the whole plan of the Sermon:

> Happy the man who fears the Lord
> By joyfully keeping his commandments..
>
> For the upright he shines like a lamp in the dark, he is merciful, tender hearted, virtuous.
>
> Interest is not charged by this good man, he is honest in all his dealings....
>
> Quick to be generous, he gives to the poor, his righteousness can never change..

So the whole Sermon includes the old and the new, the present and the eternal world as one organic whole, as well as Christ and his Kingdom come as the supreme model for happy human living.

But though this is his new "commandments" for the new people of God, also given on a mountain, Christ injunctions have several radical differences from the laws given by Moses. Christ claims a higher authority than Moses by his repeated phraseology: "it was said to you in the past but I say to you". The structure of the whole forms a radical revision of the law in prophetic terms. For it is not just the law but "the law and the prophets" he revises.

So the approach is more positive than the old law. Christ has no "thou shalt nots". He is not about law and punishment but about ways of life that ensure happiness here and hereafter. The center of the whole is the pure heart, not outer law enforced by threat of punishment. The **Catechism of the Catholic Church** (hereafter referred to simply as the Catechism) says that the Sermon "proceeds to reform the heart, the root of human acts". (1968)

That's why the Our Father is at the heart of The Sermon. It invokes the One who presides over this new moral house as a loving Father or Mother, into whose blessedness we come by right joyful living. It's the perfect prayer of Christ's new morality as inner spirituality. It says everything we need to say as his family. It is joyful moral living become prayerful family spirituality. It asks a gentle loving father to guide his children and enable them to do his will for their full and final happiness. So it is a familial rather than a legal document. It expresses what the church is meant to be, God's free beloved family, not an institution ruled by coercion.

Hence the Pope is its "holy father", Mary is its "mother" and the church itself is mother of the faithful. Vatican 11 in summing up the church as the "family" of God also sums up the Messianic community the Sermon envisages. Its overall sense is of the happiness of living as God's family in Christ, with God as our father, and the Our Father as our prayer.

Finally, the structure of the Sermon hinges on the Kingdom promise of the Messiah fulfilled in Christ. He is the "suffering servant" of Isaiah, who is meek, just and humble, a "man of sorrows and familiar with suffering" without looks or anything to attract our gaze. So the poverty of spirit, the meekness, and indeed all the beatitudes, are about childlike love of God and others in imitation of Christ in the flesh (incarnation theology). The inference in the Sermon is that Christians should be humble servants of God and others like Christ so as to rise with him. We're to redeem the world as the loving family of Christ permeating the world with his gentle saving values. The Sermon shows us how to do that.

CHAPTER 3

▼

The First Beatitude, Blessed are the Poor in Spirit

The beatitudes have a triple focus: (1) right relationship with God makes us part of his Kingdom; (2) purity within from God leads to right relationship with others; and (3) right relations with others in God leads to working to transform the world into his just Kingdom: "let your light shine before men, so that seeing your good works they may give glory to your Father in heaven". The Catechism says that "the evangelical counsels manifest the living fullness of charity, which is never satisfied with not giving more" (1973), and the Sermon's perfect way has "all the precepts needed to shape one's life". (1966)

So the Sermon is not about faith alone but faith issuing in active justice and charity. It's in that family spirit of the Our Father, of being his sons and daughters in spirit and in truth that the Sermon begins: "Blessed are the poor in spirit for their's is the Kingdom of Heaven". The poor here are those who know their need for God. They place themselves in the hands of the Father with complete humble trust. As Meier notes:

This beatitude harks back to the OT figure of the poor, the anawim, people who realize their own fragility and the illusory nature of human support, and who therefore look to Yahweh alone for safety. Yahweh's concern for the poor, the humble and the contrite of spirit is extolled in the prophets (Is 57:15, 66,2), psalms (34:18), and wisdom literature (Prov 16:19, 29:23)...The poor in spirit are those who bow humbly before God in total trust, who are willing to await everything at God's hand. They have seen through the false promise of wealth. As in each of the beatitudes, Jesus's declaration of happiness makes these people happy right now. He gives them unshakable assurance that the future Kingdom is already their possession" (40)

Most ordinary people, not aware of these associations, might say we don't see any value in poverty. Read aright, in the scriptural context Christ was evoking, that's exactly what the beatitude says. It doesn't praise material poverty but only those "poor in spirit". It says that the cure for poverty in the world is if those who cause it become free from greed.

So, with the blessing and the promise, there are the three dimensions to this beatitude: (1) humble trust in God rather than riches; (2) detachment from greed leading to right relations with others; and (3) active work to liberate the poor.

Christ says that those poor in spirit, within their core are happy, just as one might say a person is happy when his problems are gone. The problems solved here are the emptiness of the soul without God, the inner slavery of greed and the inner pain due to poverty and oppression around us. When the Kingdom of Heaven comes to fruition in all hearts, all that human suffering will be eliminated, turned to blessedness.

But firstly, we have to be poor enough within to know our need for God. We open our hearts to God not out of duty but need and love. This sense of emptiness without God is very universal. It's the attitude we find throughout the psalms: "I trusted even when I said I am sorely afflicted, when I said in my alarm no man can be trusted" (114:5-6;115;10-11,15-16); it leads to joyful righteousness. The opposite is the greedy arrogance of the wicked; egotistical pride needs neither God nor man and leads to doom.

This **Old Testament** contrast is clear in the chart below, though we must avoid rigid dualism. There are many shades in between; many who do not believe in God can be kind, just, and peaceful. Many religious people can be rooted in institutional pride as with many aspects of the official church down the ages. The key concept in the beatitude, however, is to humbly know our need for God at the deepest level, so that we can live an integral life in his power. For due to our basic freedom he can give us nothing unless we ask, he can't force his grace on us:

Chart 3

The arrogant in Spirit (Satan, the godless)	The poor in Spirit (Christ/Mary/The Saints)
haughty, oppressive	joyful in faith, trusting even in suffering
self-centered, dominating,	steadfast in affliction, kind, peaceful,

corrupt, despising the good	living in integrity, honoring all
lording it over the weak	identifying with and aiding the poor
Nazi Supermen, power as God	Christ-like servers of humanity

The second group, those who cling in need to God are like the "suffering servants" of Isaiah's oracles. They are Christ on the cross, resisting all efforts of "the wicked" to destroy his faith. They are summed up in the humble steadfast believer of psalm 22:

> Yet here am I, a worm and no man,
> scorn of mankind, jest of the
> people. All who see me jeer at me,
> They toss their heads and sneer,
> "He relied on God, let God save him!"

Yet this first aspect of the beatitude, humbly knowing our need for God, however we conceive of him, and clinging him in every storm to deliver us from evil, is also universal. It's seen in the search for and worship of God everywhere, even in primitive tribes. Like the American Indians before the coming of the colonists. They looked to the "Great Spirit" to express their own sense of spiritual need. They saw justice, truth and beauty as inherent in his creation and in their own consciences. There is a famous speech of an Indian chief, addressed to white missionaries, where he says that his faith already has more than they offer. He saw their false puritan faith as harsh law, something they offered as a tool of dominating colonialism.

For true Christians the Deity all thirst for is revealed in the gentle Christ, the universal liberator and pointer to moral happiness and spiritual fullness on the Mount. He fills the void that is all people's inner need for God. So the beatitude invites us to set aside arrogant self-sufficient pride; even in suffering we are to cling humbly to God and the church where he is to be found.

Secondly, poverty of spirit involves detachment from enslaving possessiveness. Later aspects of the Sermon develop this in more detail: "you cannot serve god and money", "lay up treasures for yourself in heaven where thieves do not break in and steal". The foolishness of total trust in riches, rather than God, is shown. But there is more than this to the beatitude.

Christ asks detachment from greed not only for our spiritual freedom, but for right relationships with others. For the root of much human violence and division is the grasping heart. The opposite just kingdom comes in our freedom from hard covetousness; it is the universal path to personal, communal and world justice.

Moreover, when we know our need for God and are free from possessiveness with his help, we are free enough to identify with the poor, the deprived materially or spiritually. So the beatitude articulates a social view founded not on limited human vision but on God's impartial justice. He loves the poor, we should do the same. A persistent theme in the Old Testament, Jesus revises this for his new covenant people. But it is also a universal view. All in their right minds and hearts want universal justice, not the harsh rule of wealthy, proud and powerful oppressors. Christ just clarifies this theme pervasive in the Old Testament and makes it more radical. For the thirst for a just and equal world without poverty and oppression and corruption, is the Godly thirst found in all the prophets, and is the almost exclusive focus of such as Amos (2:6-7):

> For the three crimes, the four crimes of Israel I have made my decree and will not relent: Because they have sold the virtuous man for silver, and the poor man for a pair of sandals, because they trample on the heads of ordinary people and push the poor out of their path..

The "they" here are the opposite of the community of the poor in spirit. Avaricious within, they pursue wealth regardless of God or man. There is always a "they" in that sense in society. Today, I suppose, one example of this "they" are ruthless global capitalists. Christ asks us to be rather humble gentle people: loving God, detached from worship of money, committed to communal justice, open to God in the cries of the poor, non-covetous, just, caring and serving the needy without calling attention to ourselves. In effect, Christians must build a just world where they are.

But the thirst for a just world is already there for Christians to work on, in ordinary people's hearts everywhere who hate oppression by the wealthy, probably most of humanity; for example, non-repressive socialist politicians worldwide. Like them, Christ says it's not good to be the poor though God takes your part. Or to be oppressed women though God endorses your struggle and ensures your heavenly vindication. All should work to liberate the poor and oppressed whoever they are and start with liberating their own hearts from greed. If all do this the justice of the Kingdom of God will come; it will take root and flourish in all areas of the world where is lacking.

So we might read a further requirement into this beatitude, international justice. There is political message here too, the Kingdom of God is different from the more ruthless kingdoms of the world but it is what we should try to build everywhere. Hence we have Christ's reply to Pilate who represented cruel Roman rule in the Holy Land, "my kingdom is not that of this world".

He says the same to rulers today: "be part of the poor in spirit, of a Kingdom which is not of this world's power-hungry and military ruthlessness". The JBC notes that Bismarck said: "you cannot govern with the Sermon" (640). One can understand how the harsh Prussian militaristic ruler might find this aspect of the Sermon unacceptable. Modern democratic models of humble accountable leadership are nearer to its political ideal. This is why so many peoples seek such free models today. They want and fight for elected leaders who serve the people with humility and integrity, whose concern for the poor and vulnerable promotes real social welfare, like Obama did in promoting health care for all in the USA, or the demonstrators of the Arab Spring did in freeing the people of the Middle East from self-serving dictators and their totalitarian systems. So this is a code for good government too: I chart its international implications:

Chart 4

<u>Nations Poor in Spirit</u>
Have special care for the poor and vulnerable
Ensure equal sharing of resources and those of the earth, Promote racial and gender equality,
Ensure equal human rights for all.
Promote a responsible stewarding of nature.

Finally, we have the promise or reward or higher motivation for all such justice in the individual heart, societies everywhere and political systems. Those poor in heart will be part of the Kingdom of Heaven, they will bring about a heaven on earth as it were, when the Messianic Kingdom comes, they will enter that Kingdom forever in heaven. The Catechism puts this very strongly by saying "detachment from riches is necessary for entering the Kingdom of heaven" (2556). The eschatological future and promise are also part of the beatitude's total moral motivation and vision.

CHAPTER 4

The First Beatitude's relevance for Today

Some might say that this beatitude's aims seem too idealistic? Yet are they not what religious and non-religious idealists alike aspire to, at local and international level? For instance, universal justice and equality were the catch cries of the French and American revolutions. Feminists and liberation theologians today also see this first beatitude as giving divine authority to their struggle on behalf of oppressed individuals, nations and women. They note the teaching's universal basis in the equality and shared dignity of all people as God's children. This is good news for subordinated women, oppressed workers, isolated travellers, excluded migrants etc.

The **Charter of Human Rights** is a living example of this beatitude's universal validity. But human rights can only come about if all recognize their rightness in their hearts and work to implement them in practice. Marx saw nothing in civil rights movements in our age except selfish capitalist individualism, the stress on "my" rights, "my" freedoms rather than communal concerns. Any purely narcissistic spirituality or morality is not what Christ is about. The beatitudes are a mandate for an outgoing community of active caring humanity. Similarly, as regards religious institutions Christ demands an active church for the poor beyond mere narrow institutional self-interest.

As such the Sermon is good news for all oppressed people. But ultimately only if rulers and everyone else are poor enough in heart to do what it asks. We require not only an ideology of justice but a spirituality of heart that drives us to action. Without this basis in active will as well as aspiration, liberation idealism may be just empty words. We cannot do it fully without God's help. That's why Christ not only gives the spiritual bases for such a moral, just and integral world, the kingdom come, but also enables it at the deepest level as divine Lord and Savior through his saving grace within dedicated just Christians.

The history of our era should show us how vital this beatitude is. For the great scourge of Twentieth Century fascism was the exact opposite. It was based on Nietzsche's rejection of God and Christian morality which he said shored up the values of the "weak" (see his works on "The Death of God", "The Will to Power", and "Beyond Good and Evil"). Look at the havoc this opposite view wrecked: wholesale genocide; the creed of the super race crushing all weaker races in its power and wealth interests; the cult of might is right. When I think of the consequences of this, I think of that book **The Diary of Ann Frank**, an example of the tyranny that worldly greed and godless power lust produces. Yet such philosophies still shape some today.

Christ's challenge to the rich young man is still relevant. The latter was a good righteous man who had kept the commandments. But when Christ asks him to give up his riches, to follow him and serve the poor, he walks away. So this Beatitude, being poor "in spirit", links with salvation offered to the rich. Christ sees "how difficult it is for a rich man to enter the Kingdom of Heaven" (Mt.19:23). Worshiping wealth as a false god, one may shut out the real God and fail to do justice to the needy. The rich may ruthlessly exploit the weak to get what they want, an illusion of happiness and the cause of much violence in society and the world, as James's epistle notes, echoing Christ:

> What causes wars and what causes fighting among you? Is it not your passions that are at war in your members? You desire and do not have; so you kill. And you covet and cannot obtain, so you fight and wage war (4:1-2).

Christ demands poverty of spirit for peace throughout the world too for there is no peace without justice. He shows us how to build a just gentle Kingdom of Heaven on earth and so also gain the freedom of the children of God. This is also in James who echoes this beatitude again in 2:5-6 and gives it an eschatological dimension:

> Listen, my dear brothers: it was those who are poor according to the world that God chose, to be rich in faith, and to be heirs to the Kingdom which he promised to those who love him.

This brings us to the final aspect of this beatitude, the humane fruits of freedom from the tyranny of endlessly grubbing for more and more money. Here again, this is a universal theme proved in literature and life. Let me give examples of that from modern cultural consciousness.

A Christmas Carol is a modern story that illustrates the universal lived truth of this beatitude. Dickens was a Christian socialist. Scrooge has served wealth and power all his life and gradually, as a result, he has become more and more divorced from humanity. He has become more and more miserable also. There is no joy in his life and he is divorced from God and his soul's salvation. Charity and service of the poor to him is "humbug". his god is money, to which he is totally enslaved. Is this true also of some today in fine houses with pads in Spain and boats in the Bahamas?

But Scrooge is shown, in visions, the "chains" he has forged for himself here and hereafter by his greed. He is also shown the social consequences of his attitudes and actions: the suffering of Tiny Tim, a figure of the poor, and his alienation from his own family. Scrooge is shown why he is loved by no one. He has even, one flashback shows, sacrificed his first and only true love for money and rising in the social business world.

But when he is converted from all this misery to poverty of spirit, freedom from the money obsession, he becomes totally different, a total force for good, using his money to win friends here and treasure in heaven. In the process he becomes one of the happiest and most beloved citizens of his town, coming back to the bosom of his family, and practicing a humane outreach to Tiny Tim. He goes from a position of miserly misery to one of blessed joy. It's a perfect literary illustration of the eternal truth of Christ's first beatitude. It is true in practice, and any man who comes to his senses from such a state as Scrooge is indeed *blessed*.

The moral of this beloved masterpiece also encapsulates Christ's view that even the rich can be saved, if with difficulty, if they use their fairly won riches for good? Nothing is impossible with God, and riches in themselves are not evil, as the church says in its social teaching. What is evil are riches won at the expense of the oppression of fellow men and woman, or riches that lead to spiritual ill health and loss of our peace of mind. Riches can make us hard of heart towards others, like it did for the Dives brothers in the Gospel. Riches can divorce us from ourselves, God and salvation. Riches can endanger us in body and soul, like they did Scrooge. And ruthless pursuit of riches can be a cause of destroying nature and the world around us. Christ calls individuals, societies and nations out of that main cause of injustice and he warns that all must face the wrath of God if their gains are ill gotten and they do not share their riches generously with the less well off.

This is the final eschatological aspect of the beatitude. The rich young man walked away from Christ because "he had much riches". Remember his question to Christ was "what must I do to inherit eternal life". By choosing to trust in riches rather than God or his neighbor, he jeopardizes, like Scrooge, his immortal soul.

A contemporary film, **The Devil Wears Prada** makes the same point in a non-religious way. It shows how the pursuit of fame and power and wealth in the fashion business can become an end in itself causing one to lose all human integrity and concern, to lose one's soul. The young heroine of the film almost goes down that road but she draws back at the last minute realizing what is really important is her soul: love, family, friends and personal happiness, wellbeing and integrity within.

I cite these examples to show that this is a universal ethic. It is unconsciously recognized and sought by most humans, even non-believers. The 2008 collapse of our economic systems due to the greedy irresponsibility of some shows the immense harm of the opposite to Christ's way, what unbridled greed can do. In a climate of Thatcherism or Reaganite economics do only money and free markets count? Are people expendable? In a climate of cutbacks the interviewer asked a politician, in a radio interview recently, "but what about making an exception for the poor". "Ah that's OK", he replied, "but it doesn't make for good economics". The Scrooge mentality still exists and thrives.

And some such extreme western secular capitalist attitudes extend to our treatment of poorer countries. For every dollar we give to poor countries today we take back nine in payments to our first world banks. If we were poor in spirit, we would write off those debts, give up some of our affluence rather than take from the poorer countries to maintain our wasteful extravagances. The Catechism reminds us forcefully that "the goods of creation are for the entire human race". (2452)

This key morality is also a challenge to the opposite communist discourse. For, as Baumgarten says, Jesus intensifies social ethics. He gives the utopian visions of social dreamers a solid psychological basis in the humane, spiritual dispositions that must be cultivated if justice is to be achieved. Justice must begin in our hearts, and our relation with God. Hitler's National Socialism, and Soviet Communism, left that spiritual element out with disastrous results. Marx obviously never read the Sermon, for it is the way to justice for this world too, to a social Utopia. But we must start by winning the human heart to justice; it cannot be imposed ruthlessly from without.

Our age showed that political or social totalitarianism to achieve justice is futile without an inner change of heart.

This was proved by the failure of communist socialism in Eastern Europe; the tyranny of inner greed prevailed in the long run; the rich communists had villas in the mountains while the area was 50 years behind the rest of the world in terms of development.

The point is made in Green's **The Power and the Glory**, set in Mexico during communist rule there, when priests and all dissidents were hung from lampposts. Eventually only one "whiskey priest" remains and he is lured to the communist headquarters by the subterfuge that a dying man needs confession. As the communist commandant shoots the priest he says, "we will get rid of God and all that and create a communist utopia". "Ah yes", the priest replies, "but you forget about sin". When the priest is shot, a young boy who has been watching spits on the commandant's revolver.

The point is also made in Conrad's novel **Nostromo**. It's set in a mythical small South American state where one revolution after another promise much but end up in the same corruption; only the power of the silver mine, the power of money, remains constant. In effect, justice can't be imposed without a deeper change of heart; otherwise we just replace one tyranny with another. Sometimes even the church has been lured into this fallacy of imposing Christ's way by political force, as Kereszty notes:

> From the Constantinian alliance of church and state to "Action Francaise" to contemporary movements the church has been repeatedly lured by political ideologies on the left and the right, always in danger of misunderstanding and distorting her vocation..(80).

Are we then to despair of implementing this beatitude? No! Christ gives the answer. It is full equality and fraternity within a just Kingdom fellowship. In this light John Paul 11 criticized both communism and capitalism in encyclicals, for both leave out the grace of God that brings justice and peace within, without which there can be no real justice in the world. Looking at Auschwitz or Stalin's gulags can one say humankind doesn't need to be redeemed by God's grace in Christ; every effort to impose a godless utopia - from Hitler to the Khmer Rouge to the North Korean communist dictator of today - has produced hell after hell on earth. This reinforces the observation in the Catechism that "without the light the Gospel sheds on God and man, societies easily become totalitarian" (2257).

Indeed, today's global warming tells us we must adopt God's way in Christ for our very survival. We must sacrifice greed for monetary gain for the sake of saving of the earth's fragile biosphere. The whole area of conservation comes in here. Man's greed must be reined in lest driven by the false god of more and more gain he tramples on the world that sustains us; but like everything else we must make the choice to serve a greener earth freely. The poor of heart must possess the earth to save it. Christ meets many contemporary international concerns here.

Finally, Christ himself is the supreme model for "the poor in spirit": He was born in a stable to identify with the poor and became an emigrant, fleeing from a tyrannical rich oppressor at home. He lived the simple life of a village carpenter for thirty years. He was a homeless nomadic preacher who said: "foxes have holes and the birds of the air nests, but the Son of Man has nowhere to lay his head". He was free from greed to serve God and others like consecrated religious with vows of poverty are today. The Reformation made a huge mistake in largely abolishing consecrated religious; for there the values of the Kingdom and the Sermon are lived as a vital example to the faithful and the world; religious take the key vow of poverty.

Christ was able to live a similar life of blessed detachment because he resisted in the desert Satan's temptation to wealth and power. The latter wanted him to be a Hitler-like Messiah riding to power on the blood of fellow humans. Satan knew that if Christ did this, he had him. But Christ chose instead to be the humble, poor and suffering servant of God and others unto the cross. As Paul says:

> Jesus Christ did not cling to his equality with God but emptied himself, to assume the condition of a slave (Ph.2:6-8)

Poor in spirit to the point of giving up even his soul on the cross Christ was raised to glory by God. This is the way to true wealth and glory. Not of course actual poverty which is an evil but "poverty of spirit", that is detachment from the tyranny of possessions so that we can be free to serve God and humanity. The remaining beatitudes carry these concerns further. Those who mourn and the meek further promote this justice struggle, the Kingdom come, but with different emphases and different rewards.

CHAPTER 5

▼

Blessed are the meek (gentle), they shall have the earth for their heritage

This beatitude also features detachment, but from the lust for power. So its promise is very different, the meek will both possess the Kingdom and also "the earth". Their humility - again we see a significant paradox - will bring them everything in the long run.

Here again Christ draws on prophetic and worship tradition. The gentle form true community and so for this reason they are sure to inherit the earth. This powerful oxymoron says that we gain everything by abandoning enslaving self-centered power. Those who ruthlessly pursue war and repression, who despise and crush the weak to gain their ends, seem to prosper for a while but that's an illusion in the end. Christ may be invoking Psalm 37 (35-37):

> Put your hope in God, keep his way And he will save you from the wicked,
> Raising you up until you make the land your own And see the wicked expelled.
> I have seen the wicked in his triumph towering like a cedar of Lebanon,
> But when next I passed, he was not there,
> I looked for him, and he was nowhere to be found.

The blessing's view of the meek as happy Kingdom campers is seen by some as foolish today. Many now link gentleness with "the idea of softness". But is softness so terrible? Are we saying "hardness" or self-assertive ruthlessness is better? If so, what does this tell us about modern values? Meekness in Christ's Biblical view is the "strong softness" of being there for God and others, putting them before pursuit of our own arrogant pride and power, choosing the way of nonviolence. We are blessed in every way in abhorring within the ruthless way of a cruel and violent world.

Christ is the model for this: "learn from me because I am meek and humble in heart" (Mt.11:28-30). His inner gentleness and humility enabled him to see through Satan's power trip in the desert: "All the kingdoms of the world I will give you if you will bow down and worship me". He chose instead to serve God and humanity unto the cross, to be God's gentleness to heal a needy broken world.

So secondly, it's in that happy healing sense that the meek are "gentle, unassuming, and peaceable towards God and man". Humility has a huge part in their heart. They are Christ refusing to let people sing his praises, telling them not to proclaim his cures. They are Christ fleeing from those who would make him king after the multiplication of the loaves and fishes. They are Christ humbly and without condemnation serving prostitutes and sinners and washing the feet of disciples. They are Christ at his passion, the "suffering servant" of Isaiah, a lamb "led to the slaughter, never opening his mouth"(53:7). They are his faithful today living gentle, considerate, unassuming, peaceable lives, imitating the humility of God in his dealings with all.

But, lest they become tired of doing this Christ gives these gentle people the promise that they will inherit not only the Kingdom in heaven but "on earth" also. Again Christ is the example. After his unassuming life of service he was raised up. As a result of his meekness he was made Lord of heaven and earth. The inference is clear it's the gentle ones of the Kingdom that will become its lords, like Christ. What seems like weakness is really the strength to rise above hard power lust to real humane glory.

History proves this at the practical level. The black people came to the USA as slaves, but Obama, an African American, became its president. By contrast, the proud and self-conceited of apartheid faded away. Mary makes that point well in the **Magnificat**. A gentle village figure, it's because of her "lowliness" that God chose her and raised her up. She says this is a rule throughout history: "He hath cast down the mighty from their thrones and lifted up the lowly". There's God's democracy in her prophecy, ultimate rule of the people, by the people, for the people.

But this powerful humility is enduring wisdom not just for this world but also for the *Eschaton*. For not only do the cruel kingdoms of the world pass away to dust in the long run but they don't satisfy the soul here. They just do untold damage as they pass along and endanger our salvation. The great literary example of this is **Faust** but it's a universal theme. The Irish version of it is **Seadhna;** selling our soul for passing power, wealth and pleasure is a poor bargain in the long run; it's the equivalent of worshiping Satan.

Godly meekness is a more wise way. As Tugwell notes, it canonizes "qualities which are the antithesis of all ruthless (worldly) achievement and success" (1). Our emptying of ourselves in love becomes our fullness of life. The wisdom of the paradoxes mounts into a clutch of inescapable reiterations.

Chart 5

> Poor within, emptying ourselves we gain everything.
> The meek shall inherit the earth.
> The mourning shall be comforted.
> The merciful shall have mercy shown them.
> The peacemakers shall be children to God.

In summary, as Hendrickx notes: "the meek are those who surrender themselves completely to God. They've broken through the narrow circle of their own wish dreams and have opened their hearts to the kingdom of God" (25). Instead of enlisting God to serve their short-sighted plans, they unselfishly and humbly serve God and the human race by giving all in love, a true and universal basis for moral freedom and integrity that is beyond even time. So there is a social message here too. Those who practice this attitude can identify with and comfort the weak, and work on their behalf. That's what the Messiah was to herald when he came, to set the downtrodden free.

CHAPTER 6

The Relevance of the Second Beatitude

The relevance of this beatitude again is in the way it reinforces the previous one in relation to social justice. To be meek is to identify with and help raise the needy. Once the meek rule the earth, no one is oppressed.

This meaningful paradox and deep rewriting of the old law is Wisdom Literature at its best. It is rooted in God's overarching moral wisdom as expressed in Isaiah; "my thoughts are not your thoughts, my ways are not your ways" (55:9). We need this higher vision. For the ruthless pursuit of power, its disregard for God and man, this beatitude says, devastates the world.

The will to power of totalitarian systems from Mao's purges to Assad's use of poison gas on his own people proves this beatitude is needed today. Hard inhumane power just kills without mercy. So for our very survival the meek must replace the arrogant self-centered oppressor of the innocent, be he Cain, Hitler, Stalin or Pol Pot.

Gentleness must replace the hard Satanic people-trampling power and ideology that haunted our age and which Christ himself encountered in Roman rule in Israel. That was enforced by the unimaginable barbarism of wholesale murder and torture, notably crucifixion.

In this Christ articulates a universal truth attested to by many cultures and the best modern media. It daily highlights and speaks against oppressive regimes around the world. But there is also a lesson there for our western culture. For the need to be ultra-assertive, even arrogantly aggressive, unfortunately, is also strong in modern popular culture, from **Rambo** to **Dirty Harry.** Yet in them we see also the theme of the weak fighting against ultra-strong aggressive oppressors; so it links with the work for justice; there is unconscious recognition of the beatitude wisdom. But this macho man, or now woman, of dominating and cruel violence, is also shown, in popular culture, to be futile and self-destructive in the long run. In many contemporary works, their triumphs are also seen as temporary.

The point made very well in that Japanese film **The Seven Samurai**. At the end of the film, one of the last Samurai, the great warrior rulers, says that their day is done despite all their show of power. But the humble farmers they think themselves superior to, will go on forever, their family and community values and peacefulness are the real enduring power in the land.

The same point is made in the Hollywood western version of this, **The Magnificent Seven.** During the film one of the farmers says to one of the gunmen: "it's easy for you to fight and die, you have no responsibilities to children, or families or community". Indeed as the gunmen live among the farmers they begin to soften and learn more humane values than their previous sense of the gun and force as the solution to everything. At the end, the leaders of the peasants and the gunmen both agree that the humble farmers are the ones who will go on and take over the world. The gunman's bullet rule is at best transitory, though in that film the gunmen do actually work for justice, if from a violent dominating standpoint that at times makes them almost as bad as those they fight.

It is vital, however, to see this social teaching that the gentle will inherit the earth as a possible way for everyone, of whatever station in life. The highest king can be meek at heart, as the humble street cleaner can be a tyrant to those around him. Good King Wenceslaus and Bridget of Sweden were of high station but meek in heart. All can achieve this meekness, whatever their station or social role. Christ himself, though lord of all, is the perfect example of meekness as wisdom. This is proved by his attitude during his crucifixion. The Old Testament prophets prefigure his meekness in the "Suffering Servant" discourses:

> I offered my back to those who struck me,
> My cheeks to those who tore at my beard (Is.50:6).

Christ is the strong one at the passion. He refuses to use his divine power to strike down his torturers, lest he be as bad as they are and endorse the view that might is right. He trusts in God even when they test him with torture, as they tested the prophets. Christ's divine meekness enables him to overcome cruelty; he is the strong one on the cross.

As such he is the model for the righteous group of beatitude people, the church. It should be meek like Christ, reflecting his gentleness to redeem the world's violence and endless wars. The church and all churches must abandon harsh institutional power and heal age-old divisions, if they are to be true witnesses to their humble servant king.

CHAPTER 7

▼

Happy are those who Mourn for they shall be Comforted

This beatitude features suffering or mourning, and its antidote the comfort that comes with Christ's Kingdom. As Meier notes, Christ tells us he came to fulfill the promise of Isaiah 61:1-3, "where the servant prophet speaks of his mission to the poor and the mourners" (40):

> The spirit of the Lord has been given to me,
> for he has anointed me.
> He has sent me to bring good news to the poor,
> to bind up hearts that are broken.

Those mourning in every way are comforted in Christ's Kingdom. There are many Biblical senses of mourning. Besides the bereaved, as Meier says, it includes "both those who mourn over the power of evil in the world, and those who mourn over sin in their own lives" (40).

Christ's satisfies of all human mourning, within and without, and this is central to his mission. It reflects the prophecy concerning the Messiah in Isaiah, quoted by Christ early in his ministry: "He has sent me to bind up hearts that are broken, to comfort those who mourn" (Lk4 18-19). Comforting mourning due to death and loss is one aspect of this. By his death and resurrection he destroyed death's power over human beings for all time.

But there is a wider Old Testament sense of "mourning" here, sorrow over all aspects of evil in the world and our lives. The paradox is that such mourning is also a blessing, for it's a form of readiness for the Kingdom and the deliverance from evil Christ brings.

So this beatitude, with the same blessing but a different promise, again has three dimensions: (1) relief of our actual mourning in the context of Christ delivering us from the hopelessness of death and suffering; (2) relief of mourning due to evil in our lives through his bringing of God's righteousness and forgiveness; and (3) comforting of the bereaved and all victims of injustice by social activism in a Kingdom church and world.

All who mourn become "blessed" with Christ's coming, for he came to "deliver us from evil" in every way. The Our Father prays for us to be so delivered. Christ brought that to those who mourn in darkness as the **Benedictus** of Zechariah says (Lk1:67-79). Haunted by death, life lacks meaning. But in Christ's Kingdom come, notably in the church, we are blessed with every higher meaning, grace and comfort, even total triumph over death; hence St. Paul's mocking taunt: "death where is thy victory!" (1 Cor.15:55).

But firstly, Christ's coming heals existential mourning over of the absurdity of life in the absence of God; the emptiness of existence and the suffering of being. His comfort for inner human emptiness is to bring the fullness of God's saving love and spiritual fullness to all.

In that sense, he is saying blessed are those who belong to my just Kingdom already in spirit: "The Kingdom is your release, so rejoice, it has come". He says as it were, "your inner angst is turned to a blessedness, you'll have Kingdom's comfort in this world and untold future bliss hereafter. I will fulfill your inner longing unto total peace within here on earth and forever in the *Eschaton*". As the **Benedictus** says:

> He will give light to those in darkness,
> those who dwell in the shadow of death,
> And guide us into the way of peace (Lk1:79).

Secondly, another door out of mourning darkness is forgiveness of sins. He takes away our burden of guilt. Our mourning there is turned to light in his new order of divine forgiveness which transforms our mourning over sin into blessed forgiveness now, and cleanses our souls for the *Eschaton*. So this is also about repentance, the alleviation of "mourning" over our sinful exclusion from the light, in a return to the joyful arms of the Lord, a healing made possible by Christ's coming. All we have to do is repent and accept his wiping away of our sins, for he took them on himself when he mounted the cross. The call to take this new saving road of repentance, and the lifting in Christ of the mourning burden of guilt man has borne since the fall, is foreshadowed in the prophets, e.g. Joel (2:12):

> Come back to me with all your heart,
> fasting, weeping, mourning. Let your
> hearts be broken, not your garments torn.

That is, this beatitude also answers Christ's key call at the beginning of his ministry, "repent and believe". Once hopelessly lost in sins, we now find infinite forgiving joy in the Kingdom.

Finally, Christ brings comfort to all who mourn in the shadow of social injustice. His Kingdom brings them the power to change their mourning over such evil by social activism. Christ provides a base for turning injustice to blessedness through a Kingdom community of preached and active charity.

This beatitude calls on the church to help all who mourn in the world, the poor, the downtrodden, the broken hearted, the blind, the deaf etc. Their liberation, as Fuellenbach says, is "both the already here and not yet" (121). The Kingdom has come already in the ways mentioned, but Christ requires us to bring it to completion by comforting social work for the hungry, thirsty, lonely, and those deprived of freedom. And all this work is energized and made possible by his Kingdom grace.

But above all, in saying "blessed are those who mourn", Jesus blesses the Christian group of the righteous, or any just group of whatever faith or none, who does not resign themselves to prevailing climate of spiritual and material oppression. Christ enables those who strive and "mourn" until its antithesis, the just earthly and heavenly kingdom, comes. As such the church is the blessed instrument of his new order, open to and ready to serve the liberation of all those in darkness by his divine power in its midst as Risen Lord, the guarantee that the Kingdom will liberate all who mourn.

The modern age - though this is true of all ages - gives much scope for comforting those who mourn due to growing godlessness, personal sin and social injustice around us. We mourn in Christ because the moral way of life of the faithful group (the blessed ones) is not being lived around us: we deplore the lack of faith, justice, peace and moral integrity in our world. We mourn and work in his power to change all that.

CHAPTER 8

The Relevance of the Third Beatitude for Today

This beatitude is so relevant for today, when many suffer in the context of what some see as an increasingly immoral and secular world. But always people long for a return to innocence, belief and godly living again. No matter how the libertine world condemns this as conservative, or reactionary, it is a blessed prophetic way to mourn the loss of God around us and seek what's true, just, good and innocent in his light. It is a blessed thing to mourn and work, despite opposition, until the dark that destroys us, in soul or body, becomes blessed light.

For in all this Christ is echoing and deepening a key Old Testament prophetic theme. The prophets are all filled with a sense of deep mourning over the decay of faith and goodness in Israel, the spread of injustice, and the punishment that is coming as a result, foreign dominance.

God deplores evil because it ultimately enslaves and destroys us in body and soul. It is mourning love that made him speak against such evil in the prophets, e.g. in Isaiah 10:1-3:

> Woe to the legislators of infamous laws,
> to those who issue tyrannical decrees,
> who refuse justice to the unfortunate,
> and cheat the poor of my people of their rights.

All must be prophets today against such oppression, not just to make a difference but to gain a blessing instead of mourning. The blessing is different in this beatitude mourners shall be comforted in the coming of faith in Christ and his just Spirit come into the world.

One of the great stories of the alleviation of spiritual "mourning" is the conversion of Tolstoy, the author of one of the greatest novels of all time, **War and Peace**. At the age of thirty he had everything and was feted as the world's greatest intellect. Yet he felt empty inside. A sense of mourning over death, suffering and meaninglessness all around him and within him, filled his soul. Then he discovered Christ's light in the Sermon, and that light illuminated his soul for the rest of his life.

He thought of the Sermon as amazing, the sure path to utopia in the world and he corresponded with Gandhi in this respect. Indeed, the latter practiced the Sermon way during the war of independence in India. So it led on to practical liberation also. Tolstoy said that others had thrown faint lights on human existence but Christ had illuminated it beyond measure forever. With the logic of a great literary man he saw that Christ's Sermon was the true and unfailing guide for lost hearts and all great souls searching for light amid the world's suffering and darkness.

A similar example to that of Tolstoy is the story of St. Augustine. A great figure in the Roman Empire, in early life he was wildly pagan. his mother Monica, a Christian, mourned constantly in tears for his conversion. One day in his garden, feeling empty like Tolstoy, he heard a child's voice say: "take up and read". He picked up a Bible from the table and it opened at Paul's words: "cast off the old man of sin and put on the Lord Jesus Christ". Tears poured down his cheeks and joy entered his heart. He left worldly ways and became one of the greatest bishops, theologians, writers and saints the church has ever known.

Here's a personal response to the gospel call to leave all mourning emptiness behind in Christ. Augustine after years of seeking happiness in vain pursuits came alive in the spirit, his mourning emptiness and powerlessness before evil led him to the lord and to active work for others in mourning, a work that still echoes for us today in his great writings such as the **Confessions**. In this classic of European literature he confesses not so much his sins as all God had done for him, all the happiness Christ brought to what had been a dead spirit before. The same is true of the **Confessions of St. Patrick**, whose words of thanks and praise to God, who filled his inner emptiness and enabled him to do great things, echo from 1500 years ago.

But as noted, Christ himself embodied this Sermon role of turning human mourning to joy. His whole ministry was to those who mourned in body or soul; he addressed their inner or bodily anguish with the real comfort of God. He didn't just teach, or tell them to have faith and everything would be OK, he healed the poor, the lame, and the sick during his public life. And he also healed their souls; for he satisfied those who longed for God above all. All who flocked to hear him were cured spiritually too. Like Tolstoy of Augustine, he lit up their lives beyond measure, satisfying their inner needs too.

This was because his heart felt with their "mourning state" without God's healing presence. No wonder Christ's heart was broken by the hardness of heart of his own people, and their indifference to his offer of liberation in every way, especially the religious authorities; they refused to accept the antidote for mourning that he brought as the Christ. His pain at this rejection finds concrete form in his tears over Jerusalem. There he longs to gather them under his wing, like a mother hen gathers her straying and lost chicks, but they would not. There was no comfort for Christ himself there or in Gethsemane but there is ultimate triumph for all who mourn when they look at, and become part of, Christ's resurrection.

If the moral, spiritual and physical mourning of all his people broke his great heart, that blessed mourning continues today. He longs to gather all people into his righteous group of happy blessed people, the Kingdom of Heaven on earth. But many still resist or openly oppose his offer of healing love. Hence some visionaries today have visions of Christ weeping tears of blood.

But all those concerned for the full happiness here and hereafter of humanity, and working in Christ to bring it about, shall win the victory in Christ at last, in the Eschaton or end time when "the saints go marching in". That is God's promise and consolation for those who mourn too at the world's evils, and at some people's willful indifference to God. This leads on naturally to the next beatitude, the hunger for right and truth in every heart which Christ both "comforts" and "satisfies" here and in heavenly bliss.

CHAPTER 9

▼

Blessed are those who Hunger and Thirst for what is Right for they shall be Satisfied

The Fourth Beatitude says something very practical, that those who hunger for what's right will be satisfied, as by a good meal. Hunger is a more elemental need than mourning, more in need of satisfaction. Lest we starve to death within, Christ comes to satisfy us.

That satisfaction comes both in the eschatological future and the here and now, through the Messianic Kingdom and promise. Indeed, it has already come in Christ. He answers the inner need of those who long in their hearts for universal righteousness, or who see where it is lacking around them, and who strive with all their hearts for its coming. Indeed with this variation the whole Sermon intensifies a pattern of subtle repetition and variation into a new sphere of untold blessedness I chart that as follows:

Chart 6

The poor in spirit = the meek = the mourners = the merciful = the pure in heart = those who thirst for what is right.

They will inherit the Kingdom, be comforted, inherit the earth, be children of God and be satisfied in Christ's coming and Kingdom.

In this Christ plays a symphony of the heart and conscience. A longing for what's right within all good people is the basis of the whole moral quest. In Christians it is satisfied by Christ's righteous Sermon way and the grace he provides to live its demands. Outraged by evil, stirred to work against it, we find the comfort we need in his kingdom way if we open our hearts to it and its conduit the church. For the Messianic end time fulfills what was the goal of that fitful thirst for moral right in the human heart down the ages and which rages in people of good will still.

So this is blessed news for a humanity hungering for what is right. Christ offers a satisfying banquet of righteousness in the Kingdom come, the Eucharistic banquet and the eschatological banquet. He says: "the cure for all you desire is come, you are the blessed ones". We will be comforted now in kingdom righteousness and on the last day when even our desires for universal justice will be fulfilled in the final banquet that is joyful life in heaven.

In effect, the universal prophetic heart is satisfied in Christ. All those raging against corrupt overwhelming odds, persecuted and alone, and esteemed everywhere as heroes, have a divine advocate in Christ. So this beatitude satisfies three basic human hungers: (1) the hunger for God, source of all righteousness; (2) the hunger for righteousness within each of us; and (3) the hunger for righteousness for the earth, the quest for a just world.

Firstly, regarding a hunger for God, Christ reveals him as a loving gentle Father. Mourning over our fallen state, our exile from paradise, he heals all that by sending his beloved Son. "This is my beloved Son, listen to him", he says at the transfiguration's revelation of Christ's divinity (Mt.17:5).

We should listen, for God's son and Christ reveals and enables the love, truth and perfect righteousness all good men crave. He frees us from the false and cruel gods we set up in our despair. This final liberation in Christ is foretold by the prophets. They rail against worldly Gods and implore people to turn to the true God and his loving righteousness, the "Holy One of Israel". They predict that a final complete righteousness will emerge when the Christ's just kingdom comes. Isaiah's depict his end-time reign as one of universal peace (2:2-5):

> He will wield authority over the nations
> And adjudicate between many peoples;
> They will hammer their swords into ploughshares,
> And their spears into sickles;
> Nation shall not lift sword against nation,
> There will be no more training for war.

Those thirsting for right in the context of corruption and widespread violence, like the Old Testament prophets thirsted, will have their vindicator at last. But unlike the prophets struggling in vain for integrity and righteousness in the land, since Christ's coming we have God's righteousness readily at hand. Those who embark on the righteous quest today have this grail within their grasp. For the sure ways to that blessedness for Christians are the Beatitudes. If lived, they heal the thirst for righteousness in the people of God and satisfy their hunger for good.

But they also satisfy the thirst for right in the wider world, for universal justice, freedom and equality. Christ in the beatitudes and the full Sermon: (1) charts the perfect path to righteousness for every thirsting human heart; (2) charts the unfailing way for the Kingdom of Heaven to grow in the world; (3) gives unfailing precepts for the righteous Kingdom group, the church, to work in his power to make the just Kingdom come; and (4) universally, the Sermon, if lived, ensures that the most anguished cries of the human heart for right are answered.

CHAPTER 10

▼

The relevance of the Fourth Beatitude for today

That the thirst for righteousness is a universal thirst is shown from many examples, religious and otherwise. For example it's seen in the modern **Charter of Human Rights** and the fight for them worldwide today. It's perhaps no coincidence that these emerged in the Christian west and are very much in the spirit of the beatitudes.

Yet many non-Christians also accept their implementation as a blessed way for the world. As they accept women's fervent struggle for equality today. As they laude universal righteous figures common in world literature who struggle in a heroic way against overwhelming odds. These crop up perennially in the best Hollywood films but also in other popular humane stories of the heroic struggle of good against evil, and the eventual triumph of right, from **Snow White** to **Star Wars**.

What Christ says is blessed, the hunger and thirst for what is right, is affirmed also in classics films like **On The**

Waterfront, which is recognized as great because it embodies the universal struggle for "what's right". I saw that film when I was young. The image stayed with me through life. I always see in my mind's eye Marlon Brando walking down that plank walkway, though battered to a bloody wreck by a mob of union fixers, walking to freedom for the dock workers he stands up for, defying the corruption of the mob fixers. So this beatitude is not too idealistic, it is present in every human heart and age.

Indeed, perhaps the greatest heroes of our age are those who hungered and worked for what is right against great odds. **Nelson Mandela** in his work against apartheid was imprisoned and tortured. Yet he was eventually successful in bringing about an apartheid-free South Africa. **Luther King** carried on the same struggle in the USA from a deep Christian perspective. He too was persecuted, shot for his pains, but all recognize him as a "blessed" man. His speech **I Have a Dream** is a perfect example of the longing for what is right that is the Christian and universal dream. He talks of all people, black or white, Jew, Christian, Protestant, and Catholic walking "hand in hand" in a world of justice, peace and equality. It is the perfect vision of the Sermon in modern terms. All such who work for the coming of a just society are "blessed", and all people of good will recognize them as such. And in the long run, as with Christ, their vision is usually "satisfied", they become national heroes. So Christ expresses a perennial and universal truth in saying "blessed are those who hunger and thirst for what is right, they shall be satisfied". Those persecuted in this way of the Sermon, are always eventually lauded as the cultural heroes and saviors of society.

But Christ also says that this thirst and active work for what is right is not something that can be imposed. Again it must come from within the just "heart" who is not happy to let evil thrive. John Lennon's song **Imagine** has a similar vision of the peoples of the world walking hand in hand in a world without divisions, including man-made religious divisions that subvert the true God of peace, love and unity revealed by Christ.

Such mourning is good for many still resist the blessed way of peace that is God's way. I suppose the greatest perversity of man is the perversion of the religion of the Prince of Peace into war and division. For this beatitude is about satisfying the thirst for right in the best human hearts, notably the thirst for peace within and without which is from God and which is only fully satisfied and made possible in Christ's grace-filled Kingdom come, and in the Eucharistic banquet's final eschatological heaven. The holiness of a living Kingdom people is its final triumph. For above all Christ is this beatitude. The thirst to right a fallen world led him to the cross. He was like the prophets before him, suffering and dying to change a corrupt world. But he is also the Christ, who, the prophets predicted would come in the end time and bring a return to the true God; and a return to individual and universal justice; final peace, truth and salvation for the soul of man.

Christ, the final divine prophet, embodies all human hopes for an eventual righteous world. He is the supreme righteous one, persecuted and killed due to his very innocence and integrity. By persevering in right unto the cross and risen glory he won a final victory for all hearts who seek right. Hence his promise that those who hunger for what's right will be satisfied.

The task for his group of blessed and freed people, his New Testament Kingdom church, is to continue that thirst and active work in the world for what is right, as his prophets in today's world, ordained for such at birth and baptism.

CHAPTER 11

Blessed are the merciful

The Kingdom "theology" of mercy is another part of the inner thirst for right present in all the works of the prophets. But by Christ's day it had been compromised by religious authorities. As Meier notes in their system the non-observant people of the land were excluded from God's mercy (41). Christ restores its universal application, and in the face of the hardness of heart of the Pharisees, he warns that without it we can't expect God's mercy.

For this beatitude is rooted in God's total non-discriminatory mercy and love. As God has mercy on all, forgives sins, and continues to love all warts and all, so should we. The parable of the master who forgives the servant's debts is a wider Gospel example of this; Christ condemns that servant for showing lack of mercy to a lower servant in his debt.

So with the blessing and promise there are three main aspects to this beatitude: (1) God's mercy for all, especially those who sin and stray from the way; (2) our forgiveness and mercy towards those who need it, our all-compassionate heart and our bringing of the compassion of God to all those in need; (3) the need to build a Kingdom of mercy - the communal aspect of mercy.

This beatitude is rooted in God's mercy, but it has a universal resonance, recognized even by those who do not believe in God. One is reminded of this in Shakespeare's **Merchant of Venice,** where Portia says mercy drops like the dew from heaven and blesses those who give and receive it alike. Certainly, such compassion is what makes us fully human. Again it is the "softness" of God, as against the "hardness" of the world. The promise however is different here, that the mercy we will receive from God will depend on whether we have shown this mercy to others; the promise is that the merciful will receive God's final merciful judgment, a fit reward.

On one level mercy here is also about forgiving those who stray from the true way, as in the parable of the **Prodigal Son**. Those who repent gain God's mercy, move from outside Kingdom righteousness to being within its fold. But on another level this too is about knowing our need for God. We must know our need for his mercy before we can bring it to others. The arrogant, too proud to seek divine mercy, often don't have mercy on others either. "Forgive us our debts as we forgive those who are in our debt"; Christ expands this by saying we must forgive others from the heart; again this is a heart-based value.

It evokes later Sermon injunctions about not asking back money loaned, or exacting interest. At the time people were thrown in prison for unpaid debts, even whole families. So another lesson is taught here; we mustn't exact what's due, though it be just, without regard for the suffering caused. A modern equivalent would be throwing people on the street because they can't pay their mortgage.

So the overriding sense of this beatitude is inner, humble and humane consideration and compassion in dealings with others. As God shows compassion to us in our need, so we should be all-compassionate towards others. Surely this virtue of compassion is universal. Natural compassion is found in all sincere hearts. **The Oxford Dictionary & Thesaurus** lists the equivalents of the merciful as against the merciless is a way that fits the Sermon: (1) synonyms for the merciful are being compassionate, pitying, forbearing, lenient, humane, mild, soft-hearted etc.; synonyms for merciless are pitiless, remorseless, unforgiving, implacable, inexorable, relentless, inhumane, inhuman, unfeeling, severe, cold-blooded etc.

Certainly, the commendation of the merciful as against the merciless is not just Christian but also universal. In Islam this is described beautifully as imitating Allah, "the all merciful and the all compassionate", one of the key names for God. Hence it's hard to understand how modern Islam can tolerate terrorism. The Dali Lama describes as perhaps the essence of his faith as "warm heartedness".

For Christians mercy imitates the loving compassion of God towards all his creatures. Indeed, Christ sets it as one of the key inner bases for the keeping of the social Commandments. If our hearts are compassionate, considerate to others, we won't steal, or covet, or swear falsely, or damage our neighbor by violence or hurt the weak in any way.

But though Christ's mercy from the heart means forgiving even the worst sinners against us, and setting aside our own rights or comforts to alleviate others' pain, it means even more than that. It means getting into their skins until we see, feel, and suffer as they do. The unmerciful, on the other hand, insist on their rights; they are detached from human empathy. People are there to be used, exploited, and punished for the unmerciful one's benefit. The latter turn their inner eyes away from the oppressive immorality of their action, or God's related judgment. They are the hard hearted ones the prophets constantly rage against. This enraged prophetic abhorrence of the unmerciful is found, for example, throughout the book of Amos (2:6-8):

> They trample on the heads of ordinary people
> And push the poor out of their path,
> Father and son both resort to the same girl, profaning my holy name,
> They stretch out by the side of every altar, on clothes acquired as pledges, and they drink the wine of the people they fine, in the house of their god.

The prophetic scriptural term for this merciless disregard for God and the poor is "hardness of heart". It's a lack of openness to God and the crying need of others that all those seeking right cannot abide. Christ in the Gospel scarified this hardness of heart in the Pharisees. Their sense of superiority over an impure rabble made them haughty merciless souls. In contrast to them, Christ says "learn from me because I am meek and humble of heart". Again we return to John Paul 11's view that the Beatitudes are really Christ himself, the all-compassionate one who meekly puts everyone before himself.

But Christ's morality in this includes, but is more than, humane law. It has an eternal eschatological motivational basis for acting thus. If we're not merciful ourselves, heedful of the needy, how can we expect the mercy of God on the last day, or at death.

Finally, as St. Theresa says, we will be judged mainly by the amount of compassion we have shown to others, especially the needy and vulnerable who look to us for help. So this is not theory then, its compassion in action that Christ calls for, non-discriminatory compassion for all in need. Above all it is plural; being merciful also means creating a community, a society of mercy and charity. And it's not "me proving my goodness" in a self-satisfied way; its humble charity where our left hand, as Christ says later, does not know what our right hand is doing.

So thirdly, this is very much a social message for today. It's active compassion from the heart for the innocent, vulnerable and helpless child in the womb about to be aborted by the mother who should be its protector and comforter. It's active gentle compassion for the needy traveller or emigrant knocking at our door for help. It's active compassion for the people suffering from famine or war around the world. It's active compassion for Tsunami and hurricane victims. It's active compassion for victims of man-made recessions and global warming. It's active compassion for aids and cancer victims and working for cures for diseases. Active, gentle and humble non-judgmental compassion must be cultivated by the just; this links with other injunctions in later parts of the Sermon.

The kindly, considerate, all-compassionate ones of the world are what Christ is talking about and commending when he says, "blessed are the merciful"; and in this he praises not just merciful individuals but a church and world community of mercy in infancy. So there is also a social and political message here. It's the nations of the world and the universal church being living communities of mercy. It's all institutions reflecting the compassionate heart of Christ and so redeeming a cruel world. And it's exposing churches of states which lack this necessary element of mercy; for example exposing child-abuse in the church as a terrible anti-Christian anti-Sermon witness.

In that respect, this beatitude is for all modern social and political rulers tempted to abuse power at the expense of the weak, such as historical child abuse in the BBC while the powers that be looked the other way. All are warned that unless they show compassion to all, especially the vulnerable in their care, they cannot expect the mercy of God on the last day. As such it is again a variation of all that went before. The community of the poor in spirit, the gentle, the mourners, those who thirst and work for what is right, and the peacemakers are also the merciful. So the Beatitude correspondences continue to mount in this relentless wisdom logic. As do the list of rewards for those who practice them with all their hearts in imitation of Christ.

CHAPTER 12

The Relevance of Mercy for our Age

We are foolish to think that the modern world doesn't need this compassion or it's impossible to do, or it's too idealistic. This is not true if one looks at the terrible unmerciful totalitarian systems of our age, such as fascism, and those who worked against it in the merciful light of God present in their hearts. **Fr. Hugh O'Flaherty** and **Oscar Schindler** are war-time examples of this, and their work continues today in such as Mother Theresa's homes for the outcasts of society. But the responses of people world-wide to earthquake or Tsunami victims show that this exhortation of Christ is universally applicable and practiced by innumerable compassionate people now, many not specifically Christian or even religious. Such as those who helped people escape over the Berlin wall, or from communist North Korea or Cambodia's Killing Fields.

Most good people, who I think are the majority of people, respond to the suffering of fellow creatures from whatever cause. People of every religion, color or creed contribute to famine relief because all of us know that compassion is what makes us human. It is a natural law, rooted in our consciences. Our natural compassion is stirred to life by pictures of starving or abused children in Africa; our simple natural conscience says we must help them.

Mercy is one of the key virtues that make us human. Shakespeare's King Lear asks regarding the daughters who abandon him to the elements if there is anything in nature that makes for such hard hearts. In **The Merchant of Venice**, Portia says that the "quality of mercy is not strained", it falls like the blessed dew from heaven, it blesses those who give and those who receive it; Shakespeare here must have had the beatitudes in mind, for he uses the word "blesses".

But this natural law is directed to greater ends and motivations by Christ. More is expected of Christians because they are part of the Kingdom of heaven, called and empowered to bring about his just Kingdom by word and action, to be the merciful and forgiving heart of Christ to the world without exception.

In this also the forgiveness of sins is, finally, a key aspect of this beatitude. The Our Father talks of God forgiving our sins as we forgive those who sin against us. The same link is made in this beatitude; "blessed are the merciful for they shall have mercy shown them"; it's God-orientated as well as other-orientated, the love of God and neighbor is linked. And one of the key ways we love is by forgiveness, mercy in the image of God's all-embracing healing forgiveness and kindness.

But this is not mercy or forgiveness in the abstract. The point of this beatitude is made very beautifully in that true film, **The Scarlet and the Black**, about the Irish priest who smuggled to freedom large numbers of Jews and prisoners of war during the Nazi occupation of Rome. He gathered round him like-minded people, a community of mercy as it were, to help him in this work. Many of them were tortured and killed ("blessed are those persecuted for the cause of right"). Even the Nazi commander of the city, as Rome is about to fall, asked O'Flaherty to smuggle out his wife and children. O'Flaherty says to him: "you have killed and persecuted my friends and turned Rome into a concentration camp, you have acted completely without mercy and now you want mercy for yourself". The Nazi commander replies, in effect, that his ideological group had got rid of God and such soft values and they will rule Europe without mercy, with the ruthless secular philosophy of power as the only right. He adds that Christians talk of love and mercy, but they're all the same, it's all just words.

Yet later, when the commander is being interrogated by the resistance, they ask him how did he get his wife and children out of Rome? O'Flaherty had smuggled them out, had been non-discriminatory in his mercy, he had forgiven even this dictator. Later when the commander was in prison O'Flaherty was the only one to visit him regularly. He became a Catholic as a result.

Indeed, when the Pope earlier rebuked O'Flaherty for his activism, saying he was endangering the church and the freedom of the Vatican, O'Flaherty replies that he knows nothing of politics, that he just sees people in need, and knows he must help them. He was acting from a humane heart, from what he knew was right, from compassion, as well as from his true Christian convictions. After the war the Pope comes to him and says; "it's because of people like you that the church has credibility in every age". The church, all the churches, must first be simply humane in this key value before they can stoop to be called Christian.

For Christ is the all-merciful example in all this. He put aside his own high state to identify with and serve the needy in an all-inclusive outreach of physical and spiritual healing, a key focus of his ministry. He went down into the gutter to lift up the poor during his public life. No one was excluded from his compassionate healing love, any more than they were excluded from Mother Theresa's charity in recent times; she lived this virtue of mercy for love of God.

A story about her merciful ministry illustrates this well. One day walking in Calcutta she saw an old sick man lying in the gutter. People were passing by, ignoring him. She lifted him up, though frail herself, and took him to her shelter for the homeless poor. She put ointment on his wounds. She washed him, dressed him in fresh clothes, and put him into a warm clean bed. A few days later he died. Some around her said "what's the point, he died anyway?" "The point", she said, "was the smile on his face as he died". All have a right to live and die according to their human dignity as God's children; Christ says in the Sermon that we must work to make real that key human right.

Indeed, he both taught and showed us this way in action during his public ministry. Christ did his many healings because he was "moved with compassion", towards the lame, the untouchable lepers, or those with mental deformity, such as the demoniacs. So this beatitude again calls for real action not just theory, or faith alone. Indeed, as Mary's **Magnificat** says (she was no plaster saint but a social reformer) we must do what God does. We must help him cast down the unmerciful mighty from their thrones and lift up the lowly. Again there is a hint of judgment in all this, casting down the unmerciful and raising up of the lowly is the way to life both here and hereafter.

So this has a resonance beyond time. Christ says that those who show mercy, who forgive, who lift up the lowly, who, like him do not break the bent reed or quench the wavering flame, will experience the infinite mercy of God also; "they shall have mercy shown to them". That's why the popular devotion to the **Sacred Heart**, which some say lacks a scriptural basis, is in fact very Christian. It is a popular insight into the heart of the Sermon: "learn from me because I am meek humble in heart, and you will find rest for your souls". These beatitudes are the gentle, merciful, compassionate, loving heart of Christ blazing with love, sacrificing himself to the last drop of his blood to raise all up to heaven and to salvation in body and soul, above the worldly crosses of unmerciful power and inhumane cruelty.

As such, since Christ is the son of God, it is also the gentle, humble, loving and all-merciful heart of God himself that we are called to imitate in this beatitude.

CHAPTER 13

▼

Blessed are the Pure in Heart

Here at the center of the beatitudes we come to the central Sermon virtue, purity of heart, cleanliness within our innermost being as some scripture scholars translate it. It summarizes all the beatitudes. In the Old Testament it referred to ritual impurity being cleansed before one entered the Temple (Ps 24:3-5). It permeates the Sermon on one level as "an undivided heart when it comes to the things of God" (Meier 4). But it s also mainly as moral purity that it continues into the motivations, antitheses and paths.

The key to all goodness is moral purity within the heart, rather than external ritualistic purity. The Sermon is about the gentle undivided heart who serves God and others humbly. We must be pure within before we can live a moral life; again one of the Dali Lama s central injunctions comes to mind: "peace within based on warm heartedness".

But Christ's vision is deeper. He says that it is out of the human heart that all immorality and morality comes. This disproves the view that Christ does not develop his morality from general principles like traditional approaches. This fallacy comes from the failure to understand the deeper wisdom logic Jesus uses and its wider implications.

The religious authorities of Jesus's day feigned moral living by external shows of virtue, but were corrupt at heart. He says to them that they must go beyond external, ritualistic, cultural purity. They were like "whitened tombs", white without, but full of decay inside. In this, Jesus addresses universal traits of hypocrisy and false self-righteousness. His call is for true integrity within, leading to a truly good life in word and deed.

So again with the blessing and promise there are three dimensions to this beatitude: (1) purity of intention and act in our relations with God - hence the link with pure fasting, giving of alms, prayer etc.; (2) purity within our own hearts in freedom from sin and corruption; (3) purity or honesty and integrity in our dealings with others; building up a community of purity in the world, working against corruption in society.

As regards purity in our relations with God, the blessing here relates to true love and worship of God from the heart. Christ says of the Pharisees, "these people honor me with their lips but their hearts are far from me". He promises that when his kingdom comes people will worship God "in spirit and in truth". This means prayer from the heart, linked to *living* his peaceful holy way and so coming before him for worship with clean hands as Isaiah puts it (1: 15-16):

> I turn my eyes away,
> You may multiply your prayers, I shall not listen,
> Your hands are covered with blood.

Above all, then, this beatitude centers on true worship stemming from right peaceful living not just professed faith. The holy place was the inner sanctum where the chief priest went to worship. They had to be ritually pure before they could do so. But ritual is no use in itself. Christ also says only the pure "in heart" will stand in the holy place where God manifests himself to man, only the pure in heart will see God and live. Such purity of heart before God in his holy place is expressed beautifully in psalm 24:

> Who shall ascend the mountain of the Lord, and stand in his holy place, he who has clean hands and a pure heart, who desires not worthless things, and does not swear deceitfully.

That's why the promise is so different here, "they shall see God". It is a more profound promise for a more profound beatitude. An authentic God focus, a heart in tune with God, through authentic prayer and right living in his light, enables us to see and worship God as he is.

We are asked us to be pure within our inmost being in the light of God, and to live in his light through true prayer, worship and charity. If the heart is right with God, then we are also right with ourselves and with the world; the peace of God within casts out all evil. Christ says it is from the heart that all virtue or vice stems. Indeed, in this respect, Christ in the Sermon offers a list of virtues and vices as comprehensive as any Aristotelian one.

As well as a right relationship with God, the Sermon also provides the basis for purity of heart in our relations with others, listing virtues such as chastity and faithfulness in marriage; authentic charitable action; verbal integrity in our speech; acting out of a peaceful heart; avoiding violence, anger, vengeance; and loving all, even our enemies. Only a heart in union with God and his perfection can build enduring values for a heaven on earth.

Finally, this personal and godly purity must also issue in concern and work for a pure, just and integral society. The whole trust of beatitudes is communal. The pure in heart represent a metonymic group called to build Christ's perfect Kingdom in the world. Hence, our duty is to criticize all corruption, and work for reform in the church, in local society, and in national political life. Our duty is to oppose corrupt politicians or immoral laws in all countries, such as laws that facilitate abortion or euthanasia. For the aim of the Sermon is to create a pure gentle world, where all are equally cherished from the cradle to the grave, a world of purity, mercy and integrity at all levels of society for these end times.

CHAPTER 14

▼

The Relevance of this Beatitude for every Culture and Age

The purity of heart Christ asks for should above all be embodied in the church. For the church especially must be the salt of the earth and the light of the world, a shining example of good works to cleanse the world of all iniquity. It must be like the prophets, who tried to cleanse their world and nation in the image of God's righteousness, holiness and humble love.

But such a search for the pure spiritual life is universal as well as specifically Christian. Indeed it is lived today still, all around the world. It is the **Buddha** seeking to elevate above all the human misery and suffering around him in a purer way of prayer as contemplation. It is numerous monks and nuns seeking that transcendent way still. It is Hindu monks and nuns seeking the pure way in remote monasteries, under masters of the spiritual quest. It is Islamic people making their pilgrimage to Mecca, and resolving to live holy lives from then on. It is Christian monks and nuns in enclosed monasteries living a simple life of prayer, humble work and union with God, living the beatitudes as an example to the faithful. It is Christian hermits fleeing into the desert to escape the corruption of their day to serve God more purely. It is St. Anthony fed by ravens in the desert, as he fled from the moral and political corruption of the Rome of his day. Christ asks us to be like that; to build moral and spiritual perfection in the heart of man through a universal witness of dedicated holy living. Many of the aforementioned show it can be done.

In this spirit all Christians, indeed all people in the world too, are called to be pure, free and at peace within, to seek and imitate the pure way of the pure heart. It's sad that often this purity is not always valued today. For it is to be in the world, yet not part of its corrupt aspects; to be free from enslaving sin, and all that corrupts us within; to practice true virtue with joy; to achieve human wholeness and overflowing blessedness in communion with God; to live lives of blessed peace and gentle faith.

For all such pure of heart, a new unique reward is added by Christ, **they shall see God.** The pure of heart, because they become like God, will have an insight into the very life of God himself. That elevates Christ's morality way above all narrow worldly ethics. We might chart its implications as follows:

Chart 7

Key virtues of the heart	Key vices of the heart:
pure worship, integrity issuing in peace, chastity result, the vision of God, seeing God, spreading love	lust, envy, jealousy, hatred, greed, anger, violence etc. result, Satanic witness risk of unhappiness here and final damnation

The greatest works of literature embody a similar quest for a perfect vision of light beyond life's darkness, from the **Upanishads** to Dante's **Divine Comedy.** The Spanish epic poem **El Cid** is another fine example. It has been made into one of the great epic works of the modern cinema. The film features a true innocent honorable knight who, though serving the king and the princes and princesses, still stays clear of all the political corruption of the Spanish court, during the period of the Unification of Spain. He is a true Christian knight, totally pure in heart, but not in a sectarian way. Consequently, in the end, both Christian and Islamic forces unite under him, to fight the invasion of a corrupt invader from Africa. The final scene, where, though dead and strapped to his horse, he rides out to defeat the invader, is beautiful. He is seen riding off down the sands into the light, with words in the background saying: "so he rode off into history, one who had lived and died the purest knight of all". He is an obvious emblem of the risen Christ, pure in heart himself, and so leading the peaceful army of the faithful to freedom, happiness and final glory.

One also recalls in this respect the poem by Lord Byron, **She Walks in Beauty**, which asserts, finally, that that real beauty comes from within, from innocence of heart and soul. The final verse is often quoted:

> And on that cheek, and o'er that brow,
> So soft, so calm, so eloquent,
> The smiles that win, the tints that glow,
> But tell of days in goodness spent;
> A mind at peace with all below,
> A heart whose love is innocent.

All such purity and beauty is in the heart of Christ, as the Sermon makes clear, and indeed blessed are those who imitate his way on earth, as another poet, John Byrom wrote:

> And, when the life of Christ in men,
> Revives its faded image, then
> Will all be paradise again.

Certainly, the key to implementing this beatitude is in imitating Christ, whose image is in every human conscience that remains uncontaminated by corrupt aspects of the world. As James puts it the key all true religion is to come to the aid of widows and orphans and to keep oneself uncontaminated by the world. Christ was like us in everything except sin. St. Paul says that he is the perfect high priest, who goes into the sanctuary once for all, and offers the one pure sacrifice for all. Free from the impurities that obscure the divine in us, one with the Father in the Holy Spirit every moment of his life, he was able to "stand in the holy place" on our behalf, and purify a people for himself, who as the psalm says, "desires not worthless things". Worthless things denote the fetishes that we substitute for God that can make our heart corrupt - obsessive love of money, lust for power, pursuit of self-centered corrupt pleasures, haughty prideful social snobbery etc.

Christ gives us the beatitudes to free us from all such inner corruption so that we can be truly free and happy within and so be blessed in every way; walking in the constant vision of God. This, as in all the beatitudes is imitating Christ himself, the purest of human beings who yet did not set himself above us but humbled himself to share our lot in every way and who gave himself completely for us as the purest of the pure. He was not pure, however, in the proud harsh puritan sense, but in the sense of the truly simple humane and all-embracing person of gentleness and humane grace within, with no sense of being superior to others, or scorning sinners. So this purity of heart is not arrogant self-righteousness, but the very opposite. It does not call attention to itself, but embraces all in humble gentle love.

CHAPTER 15

▼

Blessed are the Peacemakers for they shall be called Children of God

To live in the vision of God, pure in heart, is to be at peace with ourselves and others. This is the Kingdom goal, internalized morality bringing inner and outer peace. Hence this beatitude is rooted in all that went before.

And it echoes a theme found throughout the Old Testament, though the reference to the peacemakers as "children of God" is unique. Christ uses this for particular emphasis. Peacefulness blends the love of God and neighbor. For peace within, leads naturally to peace around us; it's the great road to happiness in every way.

So with the blessing and special promise there are several dimensions to this beatitude also, notably: (1) inner peace with God, living his peace within in spiritual wholeness or "shalom"; (2) peace in our relations with those around us as part of loving one's neighbor; (3) promoting peace in society, our country and the world, redeeming the earth as a Messianic Kingdom of peace.

The blessing already denotes this as an active virtue; for it is the peace **makers** that are praised; those who actively work for peace, those who **make peace** are instruments of the blessed Kingdom of heaven already breaking into this world. Hence the promise is stronger, for much of the Sermon is about non-violence; the peacemakers who work for reconciliation with all their might, have a special promise, they shall be "called" children of God.

It's very significant that they shall be **called** this. It suggests not only God's praise for them, but also the praise of people, for most people prize peace and Christians see it as a trait from God, special to God himself. It is the description of the Christ in the prophet Micah: "He himself will be peace" (5:5a). If Christ, the Son of God, is the Prince of Peace, then all who promote peace are like him, children of God. Hence Christ adds the unique blessing that they will have God as their Father in every way, be part of his holy family on earth, true children of Christ's Messianic Kingdom of universal peace.

All this is a huge step forward from the simple "thou shalt not kill" of the Ten Commandments. It's a new command of peace within our own hearts, through prayer, worship and union with God, and then spreading it to others. This is what makes us "children of God", and brothers of Christ, the Prince of Peace. If we have that peace within, then we will not kill for any specious reason we might invent. And once all have peace within, and radiate it to others, it follows logically that the world will have peace too. The literary logic is flawless.

But how to gain this peace is the big question. Firstly, Christ says, we gain this peace in close relationship with God. This creates the spirituality within that make peace possible. This involves more than reason, understanding the nature of peace, or a list of do's and don'ts in relation to violence in society. It means conscience in its fullest sense. It means being in touch with and personally interiorizing the divine presence as peace.

As such it involves two other factors crucial to any complete code of morality as peace from God and in God: the sincere will to do what is right, and the internal freedom necessary to do the good one apprehends. St. Paul talks about knowing what is right but obeying another law which he calls the law of the flesh. By establishing the conditions in God's light for the freedom to understand the good and the clarity of will and heart to be able do it, Christ elevates ethics to a profound moral theology, a perfected form of the Good as perfect peace.

Again the circular logic of the Sermon comes into play. We see why the Beatitudes follow one another as they do. Without poverty of spirit, without meekness and mourning until justice is achieved, without purity of heart in worship of God, then the condition for creating peace isn't in us, and so not in the world. Again the spiritual horse is put before the ethical cart.

But Christ's praise of the peacemakers extends morality way beyond the scope of rationalist moralizing about peace. For it also brings into play a whole world of older revelation. The word peace, in the scriptural sense, is derived from the Hebrew word "shalom". It is more than absence of war. It's moral, spiritual and physical completeness, healthy integrity within in God, issuing in good, just and peaceful living. As the prophet Baruch says, it's "peace through integrity and honor through devotedness" (5:4).

We find this also in Isaiah where he says of people in the coming Kingdom of the Christ: "they shall beat their swords into ploughshares, and their spears into pruning hooks, neither shall they practice war any more" (2:2-5). This theme also occurs repeatedly in the psalms, praise of the blessedness of the just man who, in tune with God, spreads justice and peace around him:

> Happy the man who fears God
> By joyfully keeping his commandments!
> For the upright he shines like a lamp in the dark,
> He is merciful, tender hearted, virtuous (Psalm 112).

So this is also peace as social witness. Christians should both live and radiate the peace of God. This also echoes themes of lending without interest, going the extra mile, and giving to all who ask, in the later parts of the Sermon. It is more than avoiding war. Hendricks describes this scriptural vision of peace as the condition of the man who "lives in complete harmony with himself, with his fellow man, with nature, and with God" (33).

There are echoes here too of conservationism, this is the man who is the good steward of creation. If that isn't a complete morality what is? That kind of morality, moral peace radiating from the individual to society will create peace in the world without fail. Again I chart this flawless cumulative logic.

Chart 8

> Peace within every person = peace for society = peace for the world = integrity and harmony in nature = true human community = universal justice and equality = all being children of God = the just man = right conscience = the kingdom of God on earth

Finally, this peace must be promoted not just in church society but everywhere in the world; we must be peace "makers" at every level. Great figures of peace in the modern world such as Gandhi epitomize this beatitude and this brings me to the universal nature of this beatitude.

CHAPTER 16

The Universality of Christ's Peace Vision

Peace is most possible in Christ's kingdom community, where through worship, the Eucharist and the Word, God's overflowing help and grace enable us to deal in integrity with all issues. But it is also a virtue found in many human hearts, and an aspiration found in most. So again this is both a specifically Christian, and a universal morality. But the unique aspect for Christians is that we can't do it fully or perfectly by ourselves. It is most fully possible when we are real worshipers of the living God. I say "real" for Christians may even promote the opposite vice of conflict, if more strongly committed to political systems that promote division; they may follow local ideology and politics such as imperialism rather than their gentle Lord.

A good example of this counter witness among Christians is the strife in Northern Ireland. There the supreme irony is that two groups, each claiming to be more fully Christian, neglect to practice the central tenets of their faith, peace and love. So true religion becomes false sectarian ideology, it itself, though claiming to be from God, actually becomes the enemy of God. Instead of being part of the Kingdom community of peace and love which all Christian churches are meant to be, a light to the world, it becomes a Satanic counter witness. Many young people desert the churches due to this sectarian counter witness, or others counter witnesses such as child abuse.

Though institutional corruption and divisions among Christians is the greatest scandal undermining the faith as peace, this is not the fault of Christ, or the faith. Nevertheless, the credibility of the faith worldwide today will not be restored until peace is restored at church institutional level also. If actual Christian witness is contrary to the message of the Sermon, the peace at the heart of Christ's teaching and example, our youth will continue to abandon it. So a return to the God of peace, not the sectarian God of our own making, is vital. In our moral weakness we need his grace to become peace to the world, and to heal divided Christian churches, for the whole world is not Christian because Christians are not Christian.

In this the churches are not just failing themselves and Christ, but also humanity. For they fail to bring the true God to all crying out for that God. Even modern non-religious groups such as the AA recognize that we need God for peace inside. We must invoke a higher power to overcome weaknesses such as addiction. Denial of that truth is the fallacy of Pelagius and of so many modern systems from Fascism, to Communism, to modern militant Secular Libertinism; but we can't do it on our own. Even the churches need to be redeemed, to humbly accept their divisive faults, and reach out for the redemption found in God and his Christ. Who looking at the trenches and poison gas of world war one or Hiroshima, can say humankind doesn't need to be redeemed.

What such counter witnesses to the peace of God shows is that there are secular forms of sectarian strife too, indeed infinitely more so; it was a multiplicity of these that made the modern age one of the most war-torn in human history. Man tried to create his own heaven on earth without God, in systems such as imperialism, colonialism, communism and fascism, and the result was war, violence, and torture on an unprecedented scale, a host of cruel godless totalitarian systems that plagued our age and made it one of the most destructive in the history of humankind.

Secular sectarian fanaticism based on divisive ideology, such as Capitalism against Marxism, is the complete opposite of the beatitudes too, the sort of ideological divide that nurtured the Cold War. It has shaped hell after hell in our age. 40 million were killed in Russia under Stalin, and untold numbers sent to the gulags, while churches were turned into museums, and priests sent to the salt mines.

Many aspects of our modern age prove the need for this beatitude. Not only Christians but all groups need to be true peacemakers, eschewing sectarian, political, national, and man-made ideological excuses for war. Again this links with the earlier beatitudes of poverty of spirit, meekness, mourning, mercy and hunger for what is right. All these attitudes must be ensconced in our heart, especially love and worship of the true God, before peace can reign; there is a logical progression of variation and reinforcement within the beatitude discourse.

Peace on earth must be based on the attitudes not of power domination based on man-made ideologies, whether of communist or fascist or western super power origin, but on peace within ourselves and active work for peace made possible by God's grace. This must be implemented in purified churches really based on his values and not on historical, political or Reformation heritages of division. This goal, shared by all people, must be reflected in the best popular culture today and linked to the need to work for universal justice; for there is no peace without justice.

But forces of local or superpower politics and greed still ferment war and injustice today, against the will of people worldwide. Whether due to western superpower cultural imperialism allied to thirst for control of oil supplies, or terrorist Pan-Arab nationalist resistance to this, the wars in places like Afghanistan, Syria or Iraq drag on. We pay lip service to peace, but fail to engender the determined attitudes within, and in our politics, that alone can bring about love, unity and reconciliation.

The will is the key. Hence the message of the angels at Christ's birth: "peace on earth, good will among men". As John Lennon pointed out in that Christmas song with Yoko Ono, peace is there "if we want it". Obviously, *we don't really want it*, or it would have come long ago. Good will, a real fierce determination to make peace is what's lacking.

Yet any sensible person sees that we dare not fail in our struggle for freedom from war. Modern secular power systems, and divided churches and faiths, are forces militating against the inner spiritual nurturing and outer will to peace needed to empower people to live the peace they seek for ideally this is only achieved by the power of God in us made available through personal and communal prayer in Kingdom fellowship. Thereby, we interiorize the Kingdom that is peace in union with God its source.

Failing to do God's will as expressed by the angels at the birth of Christ we become pawns of the evil one, and do his destructive will in war after war: from the poison gas of the first world war to the agent orange of the Vietnam war; from the Holocaust to Hiroshima; from concentration camps to gulags; from the cultural revolution in China when they ate the bodies of enemies to the Khmer Rouge killing fields of Cambodia where they wiped out one third of the population; from the seven million refugees in Syria today to the bloody hills of Afghanistan. In every age we contrive to produce hell after hell on earth instead of God's peaceful Kingdom come. We obviously need a culture of peace, a **will to peace** replacing the Nietzschean, fascist and imperialist **will to power**. The Sermon provides that **culture of peace** that the world badly needs and craves.

In the modern world we have some glimmers of the Sermon values to be optimistic about. The setting up of United Nations, though it is becoming a paper tiger today, is one example. So is the EU, set up to resolve warfare between nations on the continent, though its envisaged evolution into just another centralized totalitarian super state that controls all our lives is worrying. Why is Europe obsessed still with centralized secular control systems; have they not learned from the history of our age? Other examples of world's move towards peace are the **Charter of Human Rights**; the **Nobel Peace Prize** etc. All these potentially help work towards Christ's ideal of a peaceful world, a vision that's not just his but present in the hearts of good people worldwide.

The difference is that Christ offers us the way to that inner harmony that alone can shape universal peace, his grace within. This Kingdom come is vital for individual happiness and that of society in general for we can't do it on our own. We can only purify our hearts so that he can enter in with his peace. Thereby, we will recover our moral ground in God and he'll bring us gradually into a Kingdom of universal righteousness and peace.

The worldwide popularity of the **Band Aid** song **Feed the World,** with its cry "let them know it's Christmas time" shows popular culture potentially in harmony with this objective, and it links with Christ's mission from his birth: "peace on earth, good will among men" (Lk.2:14) This how the angels proclaimed him. This is the beatitudes in a nutshell, universal harmony heralded by his birth and the related Christmas message. And it is not up in the air; it was lived in the pause during World War 1 on Christmas day, when opposing forces crossed their lines to shake hands and share rations. The sad thing was if they could do it that day, because it was Christ's day and they knew that was what he wanted, why could they not they do it every day. Sadly, they reverted to boy killing boy the next day, obeying rather than God's will the will of remote political masters whose empires faded anyway. The living out of peace, such as the soldiers lived on that Christmas Day, defying manipulative political masters, is what Christ asks for in this beatitude. And that act of the young soldiers show it can be done.

Indeed, it must be done for without it the modern angst or alienation that is the opposite of inner peace will continue. A contrary unspiritual emptiness in our world is summed up by Yeats in his modernist vision: "The center cannot hold/Mere anarchy is loosed upon the world/And what rough beast, its hour come round at last/Slouches towards Bethlehem to be born". That beast is depicted as Mordar in Tolkien's **The Lord of the Rings.** He would destroy the shire where peace and gentle community thrives. Tolkien, a

Catholic grounded in the Sermon, saw the struggle against ruthless violence as life or death for humankind, and life and death for the environment.

T.S. Eliot a believer in the reform tradition has a similar view. He describes in the **Waste Land** a modern world of anti-spiritual and amoral robots, hollow men: "On Margate strand, I can connect nothing with nothing". He compares the endless stream of people over London Bridge to the aimless souls drifting into hell in Dante's **Inferno;** people without any spiritual wisdom or depth and so without peace within and so unable to radiate it to the world. Is it not a cry against secular modernism as the opposite of peace?

But the full embodiment of this beatitude is Christ, the Messiah, who is described as the Prince of Peace in the prophets; Micah says that he himself will be peace. Hence Christ refused to return violence for violence when they came to arrested him, saying that those who live by the sword will die by the sword. He refused to be the conquering Messiah of popular lore, rejecting Satan's temptation of Satan in the desert to use his divine power for personal gain and national conquest by war.

He carried that on into his last hours, refusing to use his heavenly power against those who tortured him. He submitted to every torture with great heroism, turning the other cheek as he had preached, being peace to the last drop of blood. Before Pilate, he made it clear that he worked on a different plane from his interrogator, the prince of a Roman power won through war and torture.

Christ's kingdom of peace was "not of this world". It is the kingdom of his heavenly Father. Christians have the role of building that today as his beatitude people. Against any call to violence made by their countries, they must follow the peace way, even if they have to suffer as a result. Only in being peacemakers, shaping peace within ourselves and in the world around us regardless of the national or other forces that try to influence us, are we part of God's Kingdom, a kingdom without the hateful wars of the world of which Satan is lord.

CHAPTER 17

▼

Blessed are those who are persecuted for the sake of right; their's is the Kingdom of heaven

As with the work for peace, it's likely that we will also be persecuted if we work for what is just. Hence this beatitude is calculated to shore up our courage in doing what's right. There is similarity yet subtle variation here on the earlier: "blessed are those who hunger and thirst for what is right". Here the element of persecution, and its relation to being part of the Kingdom, is both a warning and a consolation for Christ's disciples. It steels them for what lies in store. Christ is realistic here, the beatitudes are not easy. There will be oppositions from the world that doesn't like the just or peaceful man. His Kingdom values will threaten its greed, lust, and desire for unaccountable power. Persecution is part of Sermon living; it is a side effect of being part of God's Kingdom in Christ.

Yet the consolation is that Jesus promises that the divinely inspired righteousness that enables the good to triumph despite persecution is another form of kingdom blessedness. Its eventual triumph is prefigured by Christ's resurrection. Christ's own encouragement for those who suffer in the pursuit of right is offered here.

So with the blessing and the promise there are 3 aspects to this: (1) a deep commitment to God gives joy even in persecution; (2) inner suffering discipleship leads to active witness before the world; (3) and inner Kingdom faithfulness brings triumph here and in the *Eschaton* despite persecution.

The blessing here is meant as reassurance and comfort; it is Christ the realist and idealist all in one. The righteous will face persecution, as all the prophets did, but will have the kingdom grace and power to overcome it, and they will be rewarded by being part of a Kingdom of heaven on earth. This will bring untold happiness hereafter, but it will also bring deep joy and happiness in this world (Christ's vision is not just for the next world, a common Marxist fallacy).

Again, this beatitude is rooted in the prophets rather than the old law (Christ's new commandments are a rewriting of the old ten commandments in terms of the later and fuller prophetic tradition). It is the prophets hounded and killed for their witness. It is Amos, the social reformer, told to go back to tending sycamores, or Jeremiah thrown into a well up to his neck in mud for speaking for God. All were called, committed and determined to persevere in spreading his word regardless of persecution. And they were blessed.

This is still valid. It is the church attacked today because it opposes the excesses of western decadence. It is psalm 22 for today, where the just man is surrounded by the wicked who try to destroy his faith in God, because it is a reproach to their wickedness:

> Yet here am I, a worm no man,
> Scorn of mankind, jest of the people.
> All who see me jeer at me, they toss
> their heads and sneer, "He relied on
> God, let God save him!"

This beatitude is seen in the just man or woman of all the psalms, who though attacked physically and mentally, still clings to righteousness, and peaceful gentle integrity in God. It is the man or woman who believes through all trials and tests of faith, the one who trusts in and is ultimately vindicated by God. It is Christ himself, as all the beatitudes are, as prefigured in Isaiah (42:1-4):

> He does not cry out or shout aloud,
> Here is my servant whom I uphold
> The chosen one in whom my soul delights,
> I have endowed him with my spirit,
> That he may bring true justice to the nations.
> He does not break the crushed reed,
> Or quench the wavering flame.
>
> Faithfully he brings true justice;
> He will neither waver nor be crushed
> until justice is established on earth, for
> the islands are awaiting his law.

Those persecuted for what is right are like the just suffering servant of psalm 22. Indeed, Christ quotes this psalm on the cross. We see his sense of the man seemingly forsaken even by God who yet believes and trusts, and as a result is vindicated. For though he cried out in his human weakness, "my God, my God, why have you forsaken me", the end of the psalm was obviously in Christ's mind:

> Before him all the prosperous of the earth will bow down, Before him will bow all who go down to the dust, And my soul will live for him, my children will serve him. Men will proclaim the Lord to generations yet to come his righteousness to a people yet unborn.

This is the Kingdom promised to the persecuted just; the triumph of evil is always an illusion. So both suffering and ultimate victory is promised in this beatitude, those persecuted for the cause of right will reign in the end.

It's a psalm of ultimate faith in the triumph of the just man who, like Christ, trusts in God through all trials, and who is vindicated in Kingdom joy here and everlasting glory in heaven. This is Christ's promise to the righteous, those who persist in right despite all attacks from those they call to account shall inherit the Kingdom, for all the triumphs of the world and the evil one are illusory in the long run.

Again relating this to modern life, this is brought out very well in Mel Gibson's modern film, **The Passion of the Christ**. During the film, as Christ is battered to death, Satan is seen in the background gloating. Jesus's worldly enemies exult, jeer and mock him. But when Christ gives up the Ghost, a single tear of the Father falls from heaven and everything is suddenly transformed. Christ's opponents slink away on their donkeys, and Satan is suddenly plunged back to hell. Christ on the cross is the real triumphant ruler.

The prophets have the same sense of being hounded and persecuted for bearing witness to God and what right, and yet being vindicated in the long run through their very persistence. Though some of them falter at times, even complain to God about how they are being treated as a result of doing what he tells them, bearing witness to the truth through every trial and attack on them is their glory. As the lord says to Jeremiah when he complains to God that he is a "child" and no good with words:

> So now brace yourself for action.
> Stand up and tell them all
> I command you.
> Do not be dismayed at their presence or in their presence
> I will make you dismayed.
> I, for my part, today will make you
> into a fortified city, a pillar of iron
> and a wall of bronze,
> to confront all this land.
> They will fight against
> You, but shall not
> Overcome you for 1 am
> with you to deliver you
> - it is the Lord who speaks.

Those persecuted in the new dispensation will be similarly vindicated by Christ. Modern prophets such as Maximilian Kolbe inspire us, while his oppressors are just emblem of evil. Christian prophets killed in every age leave legacies after them that are glorious.

The ultimate example of this prophetic suffering for righteousness sake is Christ himself. This echoes John Paul 11's point that the Sermon is really about imitating Christ. He was killed because of his very innocence. It was a threat to the corrupt Jewish and Roman powers. But he was raised up as a result, and became the source of salvation for all.

Even the cynical world recognizes the power of self-giving witness even unto death. The oppressors say in struggles against them, "do not make martyrs".

Similarly now, Christians face the difficulty of doing what God says despite endless attacks by new dominant libertine secular ideologues. But here too the test of how well we are keeping the faith is how much we're prepared to suffer. Even soccer fans whose teams are struggling wave flags saying "keep the faith". Christians have a higher motivation, as Hendtrickx notes:

> In the struggle against persecution, the Christian has the ultimate motivation in the resurrection. One is joyful facing persecution and misrepresentation of every kind. For ultimately one does not do what is right for something, but for God (37).

We Christians strive for what is right, for Christ, for fellow human beings, for the Kingdom which is the perfect cosmos as originally conceived of by the creator, for the whole world's happiness, joy, peace and blessedness both here and hereafter. So the trials of the just man are the ultimate sign of his blessedness; and a vindication of the blessed way for the whole world. This gives another powerful motivation for perseverance.

Though specifically Christian, this is also a universal law. It is a truth is attested to by human experience everywhere of all faiths or none, and in every age. In our era we can cite people like Louise Pasteur who had to fight against the scientific community to get hygiene accepted in hospitals; Abraham Lincoln who fought for the liberation of slaves in the USA, and who was shot for his pains; Archbishop Oscar Romero in Central America who was killed for speaking out on behalf of the oppressed poor; Vincent Van Gogh who suffered for his art and its final triumph. One recalls lines from that beautiful song, Vincent, by Don McLean:

> I could have told them Vincent, the world was never made for one as beautiful as you.

The world was made for such. And the fight for right and what one believes continues in every sphere of modern life. It is the great ideal that "all men are created equal", as children of God, and have a right to all the same material spiritual advantages as such. Those who fight for this key Christian value, such as Abraham Lincoln, are the often the greatest heroes of the world. The central paradox here is that those persecuted by the world for righteousness's sake are yet the world's saviors.

This pain of being persecuted for the cause of right characterizes the whole life of Christ. His worldly opponents even try to kill him just after he is born; with Joseph and Mary he had to flee across the desert to Egypt and suffer years of exile. He is attacked by Satan and opposed by religious leaders from the start of his public ministry. But he is not deterred by this persecution. For it is a sign, like the prophets persecuted before him, that he is doing the right thing according to his full humanity and his calling from God. So when Peter urges him to avoid the cross he rebukes him with: "get behind me Satan". Peter was imitating Satan's temptation in the desert, by trying to persuade Christ to avoid the cross of suffering for what is right. He would have Christ take the easy way out, as would the opponents who urged him to use his power and come down from the cross at the crucifixion. But Christ chose the "blessed way" of prophetic witness, regardless of the consequences, all too aware of what lay in store in store for him at last. So should all good people, they should cling to what's right regardless, for God is on their side and their vindicator is close at hand.

CHAPTER 18

The 4 Motivational Bases

It is one thing to say the beatitudes are beautiful and we should follow them, but another thing to want and have the inner strength to do so. This section answers the why of serving the Kingdom through every trial, what should motivate and enable us to live this pure way from within a pure heart. Christ uses a series of powerful metaphors to inspire such Christian witness. Disciples must be "lights" to a world lost in the darkness of narrow self-interested ethics, atheism, cruelty, war, injustice etc. They must be the "salt of the earth". They must fulfill the plan of God, complete the old law and covenant. They must be part of the final Kingdom of God and his Christ and bring others to it, for all people's blessedness in this life, and in the eschatological future. They must practice the "more" of Kingdom morality, not water it down and destroy its radical "taste" and missionary purpose. Let's examine each of these motivational bases in more detail.

(1) Christians as the Salt of the Earth

Christ's Kingdom disciples must be the salt of the earth; not insipid salt without punch, fit for nothing but to be thrown out and trampled underfoot. Salt was huge in Christ's day. It was used for everything from preserving food to being the salary of Roman soldiers. So here we are given the sense that the disciples, going out in the power of Christ's words and example, must permeate the world of the day with his pungent Kingdom radicalism.

In the Old Testament, salt was associated with keeping the covenant. Salt that decays was compared to the fading of the faith and commitment to God within that covenant. This denoted Israelite apostasy, their loss of moral fiber, and their domination by other nations as result.

For the new people of God then, those Christ is addressing, it's also a warning that their new covenant, their commitment to the faith and values of the Kingdom, must not lapse or grow weak either. In the Greek world of the time salt losing its flavor denoted becoming "foolish". So the inference is that service of God within the new Kingdom fellowship, the code of inner blessedness Christ lays out, can become foolish and worldly; it can rot away to the foolish of the unenlightened, cruel and faithless world.

So this is a key motivational injunction. To keep being the salt of the earth is a powerful metaphor for active "faithfulness"; like the beautiful concept of the "faithful" as the apt description of practicing Christians today. One's communal witness must not grow dim, or flavorless, or without full impact. For that was the great danger in the early church. There is still a great danger that Christians might water down Christ's demands to worldly libertine ideology and so lose the full blessedness that they promise.

So this injunction of being the salt of the earth is a vital encouragement and warning also to Kingdom churches today, not to let worldly values sap the moral strength from their witness and mission. Not to let libertine values wear away the radical nature of the beatitudes. We are called not to the "less" of the world, but the "more" of Messianic Kingdom witness. We are called to higher active witness and charity, so as to bring to the world's "meat", as it were, the rich pungent flavor of the Sermon's powerful moral "salt". Christ is unrepentant about the radical nature of his call to total Sermon righteousness; so should we.

(2) Christians as the Light of the World

The theme of light also relates to this unsullied witness. It is used everywhere in the New Testament as a powerful motivational metaphor for the living out of the Kingdom values. Christians are to be like a city on hill that shines out for all other human travellers journeying towards peace and spiritual fulfillment. Indeed throughout the gospel of John, Jesus describes himself as "the light of the world". He gave the Sermon from a mountain, like Moses did for the old law, so as to spread this new law near and far.

The related metaphor for Christian disciples called to spread his blessed light, the light of joyful integral moral life in Christ, is that of a lamp in a darkened room. Christ must have had in mind psalm 112 regarding the just man and his beatitude qualities:

> For the upright he shines like a lamp in the dark,
> he is merciful, tender hearted, virtuous.

So this is an old prophetic image of the just man's role in society. But the image had special significance in the Palestine of Christ's day. As Meier notes:

> The image is taken from a one-room, windowless house, where a lamp would be perched on a stand so that its rays could reach as far as possible. To extinguish the flame without dangerous sparks, a measuring vessel would be placed over the lamp. The confident image of the city is thus given a monetary proviso. The disciples can cause the failure of their mission if they ignore others, and live only for themselves (44-45).

So this is not only calculated to motivate the disciples to live the beatitudes within, it's also about stirring up their missionary zeal to bring the light to others; they must be sparks of fire burning the world to good. Christians must be lamps lighting the world out of any immoral morass that leaves people destroyed in body and soul. They must be active, as well as interior, light-bearers. Like the people to whom the talents are given in the Gospel parable, they must not hide their light or be afraid of the "sparks" that fly to ignite goodness everywhere.

Indeed, the JBC says that by the repeated "you" and "your", Christ says to disciples that though persecuted, they still have a vital mission to the world (640). Through every trial their faith must issue in good works that bring his Kingdom to all, especially the materially and spiritually poor. Otherwise they may become narcissistic, hidden, useless lamps under a tub.

Christ provides another powerful motivation here for Christians to be missionaries. As children of a loving Father in heaven we give him glory by dynamic faith. Christ relates the blessed way of living Kingdom witness to real active love of God through loving others, notably the poor:

> Let your light shine before men so that seeing your good works they may give glory to your father in heaven.

We're to witness in word and deed. One understands then, as Stott notes, why Lutherans worried about this aspect of the Sermon (58-60). It echoes a constant call to active virtue in the beatitudes and throughout the Gospel. In the great discourse of Christ regarding the sheep and the goats, he says that all will be judged in the end in terms of active practical charity, not just faith. And Paul says that of the virtues of faith, hope, and charity, charity is the greatest

Maybe this is why many Biblical and moral scholars neglected the Sermon. It is Christ's response to salvation by faith alone. In the Sermon's perspective one is first transformed within by Kingdom righteousness, and then one transforms the world by that goodness in action; especially in relation to the poor, and building a just world. Our faith is not just for ourselves, it's for God and others. Withdrawal from the world or ignoring its immoral elements, are condemned in favor of active example and teaching. The object is to help to edify men and glorify God: "let your light so shine before men so that they may see your good works and give glory to your father who is in heaven".

This is very much the vision also in James, who interprets "good works" in terms of practical charity. An early church epistle writer, he constantly invokes the Sermon, almost quoting Christ word for word (2:14-17):

> Take the case, my brothers, of someone who has never done a single good act but claims he has faith. Will that faith save him? If one of the brothers or one of the sisters is in need of clothes and has not enough food to live on, and one of you says to them, "I wish you well; keep yourself warm, eat plenty", without giving them these bare necessities of life, then what good is that? Faith is like that; if good works do not go with it, it is quite dead.

Here too faith is to be an active quality; it saves us if we live it in charity. That's why the recent common declaration of Catholics and Lutherans, stresses not just faith but "faith lived in love", resolving the age-old Reformation dispute.

This injunction to good works also draws attention to God as the end and source of true morality in action. In bringing his light to the poor, in real practical service, we are serving Christ in a very real way; for the poor are Christ. He himself makes that clear in the Gospel, saying: "I was hungry and you gave me to eat, thirsty and you gave me to drink". It was the motivation behind Mother Theresa of Calcutta's work for the poorest of the poor.

Here again Christ's Sermon restores the old moral law's God-orientation in prophetic terms, the "more" of love in action. He corrects the external self-centered righteousness of the religious authorities, whereby they oppressed rather than helped the poor, though claiming to be godly: "unless your righteousness exceeds that of the Scribes and Pharisees you cannot enter the Kingdom of God". Christian witness today must go the extra mile too, be real active witness to love and peace.

In this, Christ is often seen as a liberal revolutionary, as against the conservative authorities of Judaism. There is some truth in that but it's mot the whole truth. Their relaxation of the Spirit of the law in their self-interest is what he opposes; their misrepresentation of the faith as passive self-centered ritualism and legalism. Christ wants an outgoing, prophetic, active faith proved by good works such as he did in his public ministry. He did not retire into an ivory tower of faith or ritual, but healed the physical and spiritual ills of those presented to him for healing especially those looked down on by the religious authorities as the scum of society.

So Christ is conservative in the radical meaning of the word. He restores the primacy of the law's Spirit in action, in the light of the new Kingdom's come in him. External law again is seen as no good, it's the heart that matters, the heart free from corruption that serves God and others without exception, in spirit and in truth. All political, religious and ecclesial institutions should serve this antithetical role of divine law beyond law, mediate it powerfully to the world in good effective witness and concomitant charitable action.

Moreover, they are not to be a dim light, like that under a bushel, but a powerful light shining forth in full strength. The motivation here is powerfully prophetic. To inspire and lift up others is the aim, and so give glory to God, the father of all. This links with the later observation of Christ that the man who hears his words, accepts them fully and really "acts on them", is like a city built on a rock shining to all in the world around it, and safe against the storms that devastate the fickle world built on sand, shifting values. So his light is also our lamp for a secure well-grounded life.

But this image also provides a powerful motivation for mission. Christ says, as it were, I give you these truth from God, hold to them and act on them, for you are to be my light to the world, I depend on you to spread my light in the world when I am gone. This is also what he says to us, the kingdom community of today, also tempted to scale down mission or to water down the faith to suit the contrary unstable night values of the age. We mustn't imitate the world, but be its light in faith, word and action, leading it to a new moral and spiritual dawn in every way in Christ.

(3) Christianity as the Fulfillment of the law and the prophets

Here we come to the core of the Sermon. Christ is not about abolishing the Law of God as laid out in the Old Testament. "I came not to abolish the law or the prophets, but to complete them", he says. Note that he does not just mention the law, namely the Pentateuch or five books of the law - Genesis, Exodus, Leviticus, Numbers, and Deuteronomy - but also the Prophets. This in itself is a major revision of the tradition. Traditionally the Bible is divided into Law, Prophets, and Writings. Christ by including the Prophets as the bases for his new commands brought a whole new dimension to law, law as Spirit, truth, happiness and freedom.

Indeed, as I have been showing, the main focus in the beatitudes is not the narrow terms of the Law. The focus of Christ's new law is the spiritual "more" of the dynamic prophetic spirit, which is sent to renew the face of the earth.

His new law is not just a succinct summary and beefing up of the essentials of the old law, originally called "teachings", for another reason. For the complex of laws in the original books of the law, especially in Numbers, would be impossible to require for the new world or universal Kingdom of God Christ is founding. Rather he rewrites the teaching or core of the old law, the Decalogue, in the light of his reality as the Christ, the final prophet, the Son of God, who completes the revelation of God to the world in an end-time law and covenant for a new universal Kingdom people.

In this, by including of the vast Prophetic corpus in this new moral teaching of the Sermon, he makes possible both a simplification, and yet a huge extension of the law. For in the prophets the whole radical Messianic vision and purpose is prefigured and outlined. It will be a new era of perfect universal justice that the Christ will preach and bring into being, beyond the more limited and ultimately unnecessarily detailed clan morality of the old Israelite dispensation.

Moreover, the prophets brought out more the spirit of the law in their inspired teachings and looked always to the more perfect law of the Messianic end-time. That's what Christ achieves in the Sermon and the gospel in general. He is the Christ. His prefigured Kingdom, prefigured in all the hopes of the prophets for a just world, has come.

The two key phrases in the Sermon then, in relation to the old Law, are, (1) "complete the law", teasing out key interior dispositions needed for its real implementation, stripping it down to its spiritual essentials for an international audience, its "completion" in prophetic Messianic end-time terms; and (2) in the process achieving "the purpose of the law", defining the reason or motivation for his perfected rewriting of it, namely a new simpler, yet in other ways more radical version of the law for the end-time Kingdom of God on earth that he has come to establish, a Kingdom empowered by his resurrection.

In this respect we might ask what is the "purpose" of moral law at all for is not that what Christ also asks? What was the "purpose" of the old law that Christ wants to restore and revise? Obviously, the purpose of the old Law was to free those who had been physically freed from Egypt, free them in a deeper moral and spiritual way as God's people.

The "purpose" of Christ's new law is even more so. It's calculated to make people freer and happier, not to burden or restrict them by minute strictures. For it was out of love that God showed the Israelites, through the law, how to have a better life. It's to hammer this point home for the new Israel that is the universal church, that Christ uses the term "happy" to preface all his new laws. He came that we may have life in its fullest glory. The purpose of his new law on the Mount is the fullness of human happiness.

For the purpose of the law in his day, through the Pharisees, had been reduced to burdensome rules, such as churches tended to impose in the past in the strict Puritanism that followed the Reformation and Counter Reformation. That missed the purpose of the law, to make people happy, free and joyful members of the Kingdom of God's blessed ones, free from the darkness, enslavement to evil and the pain of those without divine guidance or grace.

So conscious of getting rid of the burdensome additions Christ dumped the detailed paraphernalia of the Old law, which condemned the religious authorities of his day to endless detail, often far from its spirit. Christians since Christ should just as happily set aside these burdens of the law and enjoy the full freedom of the children of God which St. Paul shows is our newer and fuller inheritance in Christ.

Secondly then, it's in this prophetic end-time sense that the Sermon is the "completion", of the law. He restores its purpose by moving away from a "thou shalt not" approach altogether. But he also "completes" the Old Law by radicalizing its demands and so bringing a deeper freedom and happiness to the new people of God. The external ritualistic approach of the Scribes and Pharisees, whereby they kept a vast array of detailed external aspects of a very cumbersome law but ignored its spirit is what Christ is moving beyond. But he also makes the law more challenging, a sophisticated "more" in the Sermon. To achieve the "purpose" and "completion" of the old law in a relatively short Sermon, and yet add more radical Messianic mission aspects, is an amazing achievement.

(4) Christians as Christ's New Kingdom of Heaven on Earth

This is the final and central motivation of the Sermon. Christ urges us to be active partners in his end-time Messianic Kingdom. This was foretold by the prophets as a perfect kingdom of justice and truth, as in Isaiah's wonderful poetic vision. It would be a utopian world where the lion would lie down with the lamb. The Sermon then is such a prophetic utopian charter for a righteous Kingdom group, the new people of God he is to establish. The fact that he mentions "unless your righteousness exceeds that of the Scribes the Pharisees you will not enter the Kingdom of heaven" makes that clear.

"Kingdom" here must not be seen in worldly power terms but more in terms of the rule of love and truth. Christ was its king on the cross of total love and service. That's how his followers must also reign in the world; for the Kingdom is really about the reign of a God of love in our lives and in the lives of all his children in the world for their greater good.

It's for happiness in every way, then, that we should be part of his end-time glorious Kingdom of God on earth, the perfect Way. The religious authorities of the day kept the

Law to the letter, yet they were very far from that Kingdom; like many today they didn't even understand what he was all about or pretended they didn't understand. Caught up in law as burdensome detail or merely cultural norms they could not see or accept his freeing vision; the real achieving of the "purpose" and the completion of the law is our complete integrity, freedom and happiness.

The more active opponents of his Kingdom vision must have had some inkling of what he was about, the tearing down of their edifice of empty conformism, or they wouldn't have opposed him so vehemently. Christ was unashamedly turning their rigid religious world upside down as God's final prophet and promised Savior. They didn't like it. Their willful resistance was what he describes as "hardness of heart", they didn't want to accept what in their hearts they knew was true. They closed their hearts to the truth, lest they should believe, and have to give up their power, and corrupt riches. The same thing happens in every age, even within the church.

Yet Christ makes it clear that his new way is not a tearing down of Divine Law in its essence, rather the opposite, it is restoring its original spirit. This paradox accounts for the complexity of the section of the Sermon leading up the antitheses. Here is the complete law we're asked to keep; if we do so we will achieve the purpose of the law, to bring God's values to earth, to create a happy Messianic utopia.

The key is not to harden our hearts but open them to the Kingdom; for we cannot achieve the Kingdom by ourselves. Only by being humble and poor enough in spirit to accept it will we gain its joys. All Christians have a share in that task through their baptism, the new entry gate to the happy righteous Kingdom group of Christ, beyond all law and yet keeping all law in Christ.

CHAPTER 19

▼

The Antitheses

The Sermon's series of powerful literary antitheses spell out more fully the inner Kingdom morality as against self-serving legalism, and what it means for everyday life. The beatitudes and motivations lay down the key principles, and the antitheses tease them out in everyday terms.

By antitheses I mean significant contradictions of the old law in new prophetic terms. For example, Christ mentions how it was said in the past that a man could divorce his wife. But he says that a man who does so commits adultery. Christ deliberately sets his new vision as a perfection of the old law, especially the Ten Commandments. But he also fulfills the law and commandments in these antitheses. For example, he both proves the wisdom of the old law in relation to marriage by the Genesis quote and radicalizes it by excluding divorce. In the beginning, he says, God made us male and female, and decreed that a man must leave his parents and be joined to his wife so closely that they become one flesh; "what God has joined together, man must not put asunder". So there is both keeping and completion of the original law in the antitheses.

It's in that sense that Christ asserts that he is the ultimate interpreter and reviser of the law, even greater than Moses, to whom the five books of the law were originally attributed. So time and time again in the Sermon the phrase "it was said to you in the past" is followed by the stress on his unparalleled authority as moral teacher: "but I say to you".

The First Antithesis - A Return to the Theme of Peace

Christ's antithetical re-invigorating and interiorizing of the law starts with a basic tenet of the Decalogue: "thou shalt not kill". The theme of Peace is huge throughout the Sermon, returned to again and again, because it is central to its message. It envisages peace within through union with God in love, and so also peace on earth as a result. So here Christ returns to this key theme. He points out that before we can achieve peace we must address the violence within our hearts. Again in the circular organic literary logic of the Sermon this links with and expands all that went before - the prophetic beatitude calls to inner freedom from domination and greed, to peace, mercy, meekness, not returning evil for evil, striving with heroism for what is right. The first antithesis is really an elaboration on the central beatitude concerning peace, the prophetic vision of the gentle, peaceful and just man.

Once more the focus is on the heart. Like the prophets he says we must start by correcting the inner causes of killing and maiming, what causes the lack of peace in our hearts - anger, hatred, calumny, verbal abuse of others, law suits, resentment, feuding, revenge, desire for power. By outlining antidotes for inner evils that spark interpersonal and communal strife, Jesus sets the basis for the peaceful purity of heart listed in the Beatitudes.

Repressed anger is psychologically unhealthy but that's not what Jesus is condemning. As the JBC notes: "we must acknowledge our angers but not act them out in rage or killing or other violence" (642). Indeed, righteous anger is part of the earlier beatitude of striving for what is right.

Jesus's anger in cleansing the Temple is this type of "mourning" or righteous anger: "my house shall be called a house of prayer, but you have made it a den of thieves" (Mk.11:17-18). Christ overturned the tables of the money changers because they were using the Temple to exploit the poor coming to buy Temple offerings. True worship in the Kingdom, union with God in authentic, personal and communal prayer, starts with a just heart.

Hence the link in this antithesis is with true worship. Worship of God must be preceded by charitable living, if we are to meet God and see God through our worship. This links with the earlier beatitude also of purity of heart entering the sanctuary. Bringing our offering to the Temple or today to church we cannot worship God or achieve grace and salvation if we've resentment or hatred towards our brother in our hearts; the worship becomes a mockery. Worship is meant to reflect our love of God, of which peace towards others is an integral part. Christ restores the essential link between love of God and love of others.

So reconciliation with others is an integral part of preparation for true worship of God; hence the entrance penance rites to begin mass today. So is settling law cases out of court, another practice mentioned in this antithesis. It resolves the bitterness that results from pressing the law too harshly. Such use of law creates inevitable resentment and trouble for the future, for us and others. Another aspect of moral logic is clear here too: even when we press our case too fully and lose, our opponent who wins won't be ready to be lenient with us in future; "you showed no give and take, no mercy, so why should we", they might say.

This links with mercy again, not seeking to the last jot what we are entitled to; the law must always be tempered by mercy. In this case, we moderate our demands in the interests of peace with all and our eschatological future lest we languish in prison forever: "Amen I say to you, you will not get out until you have paid the last penny".

The link with peace is clear, unless we are at peace with others we cannot expect to enjoy the peace of God in prayer. And unless we promote reconciliation in our relational, legal and other everyday activities here we may not be at peace for eternity. The role of the gentle, reconciling and compromising man of the prophets is set before us as the basis for peace in every way.

Insulting others, the destruction of peace with them, falls into the same category. Calling others fool, probably empty-headed is the true translation, or "renegade", also stirs them up against us; insulting name calling is hardly a recipe for a peaceful world. It is the opposite of that gentleness and respect for others which is the essence of the beatitudes as a code of peace. So all this follows the hidden and deeper literary divine wisdom logic of the whole. All the beatitudes and the antitheses reinforce one another in a kind of circular logic of literary reinforcement and expansion that stretches to eternity and beyond as it were, and situates Christ as the supreme moral teacher, fulfilling the old law. Again we might chart this as follows:

Chart 16

<u>The narrow limited old law</u> <u>The fuller new law</u>
"thou shalt not kill" - no anger, insults..etc.
A basic law for a tribal people, A comprehensive new law
addressing basic social order healing the causes of all
individual and communal
strife

Beatitude expanded - blessed are the peacemakers "I say to you do not even be angry with your brother"

Yet there is nothing extraordinary about this new approach. It is just common sense. There is a need to address the root causes of all violence if it is to be eliminated everywhere. And compromise and negotiation is needed when there is war. Again, this is not only an imperative for Christians; it is a universal norm found in most cultures. How many times do we hear people throughout the world say of feuding groups, "they should come to the negotiating table". And how many times does the UN plead with warring factions throughout the world to come together and seek a compromise. All this echoes Christ's advice: "be reconciled with your brother", lest things get steadily worse. For if people stand on their violent reactions, and refuse to budge, here is no possibility of ending war. The need for a coming together of minds in a spirit of real give and take is the only way forward.

Daily, reconciliation processes in Northern Ireland and elsewhere highlight this fact. And obviously, doing this before war ever breaks out is even more vital, offsetting the cycle of violence before it begins. I mentioned Lennon's song **Imagine** as embodying this ideal, but it is also there in the pacifism of other great modern heroes such as Daniel O'Connell in Ireland. Indeed, the **United Nations** was set up for that purpose, to mediate in and offset national conflicts. And the modern world still needs this approach. For though the modernist movement foresaw a world of endless progress and an end to war, sadly, the Twentieth Century has in fact been one of the most war-torn in History, with two terrible world wars, and endless smaller wars and genocides. That is continuing into the 21st century; for example with the terrible wars now in Iraq and Syria that have spawned seven million refugees. Christ's recipe in the Sermon, outlining the ways to offset the causes of national or communal strife is eternally relevant.

Christ didn't just preach this doctrine, he lived it. Christ was the meek and mild one who offered his back to those who were beating him, refusing to return violence for violence. He displayed righteous anger at times such as in the cleansing of the Temple. Yet his overall refusal to return evil for evil, violence for violence, is the embodiment to this antithesis. This was because his role as the Christ was to be the Prince of Peace (see Isaiah 62:1-5), the prophetic role also given to him as the promised Christ in Isaiah 2:1-5:

> He will wield authority over the nations, and adjudicate between many peoples; they will hammer their swords into plough shares, their spears into sickles.
> Nation will not lift sword against nation, there will be no more training for war.

Christ is the Prince of Peace, mainly because he tells us how to heal all the causes of violence in the fallen human heart. By living this way, living the beatitudes, loving even his enemies on the cross, he gave an example of the Old Testament figure of the perfect just man whose very way of life is peace and who therefore worships God in spirit and in truth. He is **shalom**, the just man who not only avoids war but is perfectly in harmony with God, his fellow man and with the world of nature around him.

If one establishes a society of such individuals, one need have no fears for its future. It is not based on passing human ideologies which are necessarily partial leading to conflict because of their irreconcilable "them" and "us" biases, their demonizing of the "other" to maintain their hegemony (e.g. liberal against conservative now). They pass because the unconscious other they suppress inevitably rises up to undermine them and expose their unsatisfying partiality (e.g. the rise of Trump against the "liberal" hegemony in 2016?). By contrast, the church is not based on divisive human ideology but on a relationship with the living God. It embodies the timeless wisdom of God and his Christ; only this can explain why it has survived thousands of passing and opposing arrogant human ideologies and rolled past them like a river. Though it may be down for a time, it always rises again like its risen Lord and continues its expansion, for Christ has promised to be with it until the end of time and that the gates of hell will not prevail against it. So it is bound to roll past present opposing secular ideologies also in the long run, their partiality is the denial of the necessary spiritual eternal dimensions of humanity. No society with that degree of partiality can survive or be a holistic entity. All is passing and partial other than the wisdom of God and his Christ as embodied in such as the Sermon; that is eternal truth.

CHAPTER 20

▼

The Second Antithesis: Healthy Sexual Attitudes and Relations

This is perhaps the most controversial part of the Sermon for today. The attitude now seems to be at times that almost anything is permissible in this area. The second antithesis extends Christ's radical revision of the Ten Commandments to the area of sexual relations with a clear definition of what is right and wrong in this respect. Yet it must be said that the sixth and ninth commandments are rewritten by Christ in real positive theological terms. For, as with his other injunctions, Jesus deals with basic pure-heart attitudes in this area too. If lust is allowed to reign in our hearts it's no use saying, "thou shalt not commit adultery", or "thou shalt not covet thy neighbor's wife". His central vision in the Sermon is of a morality that's not external law and morals but that comes out of a pure heart. In this antithesis again he goes to the root causes of sexual immorality and violence, uncontrolled or disordered inner desires. He says that "whoever looks at a woman lustfully has already committed adultery with her in his heart". We're back to the beatitude, "blessed are the pure in heart".

Rationalists might see avoiding lustful glances as extreme but it must be seen as very logical in the context of Christ's whole Sermon theme; all goodness or evil starts in the human heart. Only right attitudes within can lead to external righteousness in this area too; for happiness, virtues of chastity and modesty must be cherished. The Catechism points out "modesty protects the intimate center of the person" (2533), and adds elsewhere "there is connection between purity of heart, of body, and of faith (2518).

Christ's reasoning is very consistent and valid. One can't be pure in heart without controlling bludgeoning inner sexual evils from the outset. Indeed, for those who might find this objectionable he is unapologetically uses deliberate hyperbolic exaggeration to hammer the message home.

For here Christ's concern is for the protection of men, women, and children from destructive sexual aberrations. The acting out of disordered or perverse sexual desires must be redeemed in Christ's Kingdom, and the innocent sexuality of the original creation restored. He is the spiritual physician, curing the root cause of ills in this area.

In this light Christ is severe on anyone who gives scandal to the young or sexually uses them for perverse pleasure. In the Gospel he speaks with "mourning" anger against those who scandalize children. He doubtless had sexual sins against the young in mind when he says of abusers: "It was better for them that a millstone was tied about their necks and they were drowned in the depths of the sea" (Mt.18:5-7). A similar reaction and outrage is seen even in modern permissive societies over pervasive instances of child abuse.

In our world today revelation after revelation of such abuse shock us into asking where we are going as a modern society in relation to sexual license. Is the libertine approach of modern society to blame for increasing instances of sexual exploitation of the young and vulnerable? Is the turning of a blind eye to sexual excess by society and to promiscuity in general really healthy? Can we express shock at sexual perversions abroad if our general attitude to sexual practices is ultra-permissive? These questions need to be asked.

One can understand why Christ's reasonable approach can seem severe to a liberal society. To moralize at all in this area has become a no-no because of the excessive moralizing of the past, especially in Puritan societies: witch hunts, moral segregation etc. People abhorred the way sexual morality was used as an abuse of power by church and state alike; even normal outlets for sexual expression were closed. Now do we go to the other extreme, afraid to offer clear Christian guidelines lest they encroach on freedom in the sexual area. But what Christ says stands. If improper sexuality is allowed reign in the human heart it will inevitably become a problem in society and the most vulnerable will suffer most.

In fact in this antithesis and in the Gospel in general, Christ charts a middle way between puritan prudishness in sexual areas on the one hand and excessive promiscuity on the other. In that respect again the Sermon is the perfect combination of infinite challenge and infinite compassion.

Christ says that "sinners and prostitutes" will enter the Kingdom of heaven before the hard hearted religious authorities. He has a soft spot for human weakness in this area, saying also of the woman who washed his feet that her many sins were forgiven because she loved much; the Pharisees would have condemned her out of hand for her "loose" ways.

Similarly, he says of the woman caught in adultery; "let he who is without sin cast the first stone". Christ practices the non-judgmental teaching of the later Sermon.

But he also says to the woman, "go and sin no more". He also calls to conversion the woman at the well who has had seven husbands and the man she is living with now is not her husband. Christ does not condone sins of a sexual nature. But in refining the old law's condemnation of adultery and unmitigated lust, it is not law but sexual relations as expressions of real love that he is defending (the sins of the "loose" woman who washed Christ's feet are forgiven by him because she has "loved much"). It's for the same reason that he insists on the ideal of a life-long and faithful marriage. In effect, sexuality at its best must be rooted in real inter-personal closeness. What he condemns are mainly the perverse hard hearted types of sexual sins that center purely on self and pleasure and harm others, especially women and the most vulnerable. He hints that the Scribes and Pharisees were of this type; whited graves on the outside, adhering to external law, but on the inside full of corruption. He is less hard on the "innocent" sexuality stemming from human weakness of the woman caught in adultery, whose sexual sins did not stem from a corrupt heart like that of the Pharisees. They would have him condemn her to death according to the letter of the law but he points out, "let he who is without sin casts the first stone".

They go away when he starts writing in the sand, showing he knows they are sexual sinners in a more serious way than the woman, and they know that he knows. There are echoes of the "old men" who condemn Susanna in the **Book of Daniel**. Kingdom righteousness is more than hypocritical judgment.

Yet though Christ doesn't condone rigid condemnation of the sexual sinner - like the church he always loves and forgives the sinner knowing no man or woman is perfect - yet his insistence in the Sermon on the joy and inner freedom of right sexual attitudes in the heart still holds. The blessedness of the right way for here as well as hereafter is not just in avoiding adultery but in healing the uncontrolled inner lusts that lead to adultery and impurity of every kind. Not coveting one's neighbor's wife, the old law, becomes avoiding all inner covetousness in the sexual area, the real cure for adultery. To take one's neighbor's wife or husband outside of marriage is to violate natural justice and show lack of love for others. This follows the heart logic of the whole Sermon; as the cure for violence is healing its causes within the heart so it is with sexual evils. Our happiness and society's good is in sexual integrity within leading to outer sexual integrity, leading to persevering in true love and authentic marriage and to avoiding anything that uses or causes deep hurt to others. Thereby a healthy society is built; it all fits together.

Sexual morality or Christian purity of heart and chastity in this area is again not about law. It's about happiness for the individual and the world. A healthy sexuality within, and marriage faithfulness built on deep love, is the way to true happiness. Moreover, this is the Kingdom come. The salvation of one's soul means curbing the sexual lusts that harm our relationships and society's unity, children's need for a stable loving home environment, and our own soul's health both for happiness in this world and unto eternity.

The special aspect of this antithesis is its exaggeration for effect; a sign of how seriously Christ views these issues. Hence the hyperbolic saying about plucking one's eye out if it gives scandal. The lustful eye, here a metaphor for inner uncontrolled lust, must be plucked out not in the literal but the spiritual sense of purifying the heart. We are back to the beatitudes again. Whatever undermines integrity in the sexual area is to be avoided for it can eventually contaminate the whole heart. This gives the lie to those who say Christ gave no moral guidance in sexual matters.

Sure, he didn't write a manual listing all the sexual sins, but he gives all the main pure inner attitudes we need to be healthy sexual beings. In this he says, like in everything else, like with disease prevention, we must start by curing the life practices and avoiding the contexts that cause sin.

Christ says that indulging disordered sexual desires without restraint visually from within often leads to indulging them also in actuality. The "hand" or act follows from the lustful wish. Both must be avoided but avoiding the cause is more urgent. He is not really saying that we should cut off our hand if it causes us to sin. This is deliberate hyperbole of literary logic. For sexual integrity one must cut out all that if uncontrolled will lead eventually to adultery and undermining of real love. To really drive this home Christ like a good teacher uses exaggerated metaphors.

Hence we see other hyperboles in this teaching. We must pluck out the eye if it causes us to sin because it's better to go blind to sexual temptation of a sordid nature to save our souls than to go with two eyes into eternal damnation. There is an eschatological dimension here. He is not exhorting us to really tear out our eye if it leads us to lust; he just emphasizes the gravity of sexual evil as a threat to our souls: "if your eye causes you to sin tear it out".

The greater good of our souls and the priority of our eternal salvation is affirmed over false and perverted sexual pleasures that can lead, at death, to our souls being cast forever into the darkness where there is "weeping and gnashing of teeth" and where their worm never dies. This seems to confirm modern theological theories that our lot in the next world is not God punishing or rewarding us but more the effects of our own choices and actions in this world carried on into the next. The corrupted heart will choose the corrupt way in the afterlife also and this is hell. As a man lives so shall he die; the eternal separation from God is our choice and it is hell because it is an eternal separation from all that is good, right and loving.

That punishment has already begun here. There is "no rest for the wicked" in this world either. I think of lords of the sex trade who, in our capitals, kill each other and pervert our youth for money and pads in Spain. The horror of people and child sex trafficking are other cases in point. What use are riches got from crimes if the criminals lose their souls thereby and have consciences that know no peace? The point is made well at the end of the **Godfather** films.

Christ's warning about the personal, social and spiritual dangers of sexual evil is relevant for today when we see uncontrolled sexuality becoming a major problem leading to other evils such as wholesale abortion, rising instances of sexual disease, the breakup of the family because of infidelity and adultery, the downgrading of lasting marriage, the increasing prevalence of rape, the abuse of women and children in the home, the trafficking of young girls and boys from abroad for the sex trade, the turning of sex into a sordid industry, the internet pornography industry that includes child pornography and so on. So this is very much a moral message for our age; we must clean up our act as individuals and as a society lest our children suffer grievously in the long run. In all this Christ echoes the condemnation of social corruption due to sexual sins that one finds in the preaching of prophets such as in Jeremiah:

> Oh! Your adulteries, your shrieks of pleasure,
> your vile prostitution!
> On the hills, in the countryside,
> I have seen your Abominations.
> Woe to you, Jerusalem, unclean still!
> How much longer will you go on like this?

By comparison Christ's appeal for purity in sexual matters is mild. But he does set ideals before us of faithful love and marriage which lead on to the third antithesis.

Finally, let me add that Christ himself was not the sexless figure he is often depicted as. He was close to women friends such as Martha and Mary, and in the garden after the resurrection he had to tell Mary Magdalene not to "cling to" him; she must have been used to doing so. It is clear from the Gospels that he just chose a celibate life "for the sake of the Kingdom" not for prudish reasons. Celibate priests and religious do the same in imitation of him and the purity of heart and service he embodied. The imitation of Christ in this area, and the priest is in *Persona Christi*, is a great and irrefutable argument for priestly celibacy.

CHAPTER 21

The third antithesis: enduring love and marriage fidelity as images of God's faithful love

The third antithesis is again controversial in libertine modern terms. Christ situates the interior basis for marriage and family morality in a great inner spiritual idealism - radical life-long love and faithfulness. In a modern sense I suppose Christ could be considered an ultra-romantic. He says that in his perfect Kingdom there should be no watering down of married love or marriage commitment in the interest of cynical worldliness. But this teaching is more than romance. It stems from a deeply-rooted theological and eschatological vision. It's the "more" required of those who belong to the new Kingdom of heaven on earth Christ came to establish.

For this new Kingdom witness people must have higher standards if they are to be the light of the world. They must imitate God whose love is faithful forever. The Kingdom is about following that blessed way to happiness here and hereafter. This is arguably urgent now in the context of what some see as an increasing prevalence of messy divorce, family breakdown, abandonment of marriage altogether, one night stands, single multi-parent families etc.

This antithesis is about the contrary road to real happiness. Christ says: happy are the true lovers, the enduring lovers and the married lovers until death. They will be happy together here and with God for all eternity. For the senses of this antithesis are many: that real love is from God, destined, deeply rooted, and always orientated towards the good of the other, "what God hath joined together let no man put asunder"; that true love and marriage are made in heaven; that it's God who brings true lovers together; that it is only in living out the gift of true and enduring love that people can truly be at peace within, with each other, sexually fulfilled and happy mothers and fathers. In effect this antithesis says that a world of happy fathers, mothers and children living in faithful love in a happy home full of love is the Kingdom come.

All this may seem over-idealistic for today. But for Christians the overflowing grace of Christ and that of the new redeemed Messianic order of creation makes it more than achievable. It is part of the suffering "more" of the Kingdom Christians must serve selflessly.

By contrast, passing sexual use or abuse of the other is a travesty of this ideal. That's why things like rape are so evil. They turn what is holy into violence. They turn love into power and cruelty. So all this links with the previous antithesis, it's about peace within and suffering in doing what is right, not violent, cruel or cynical use or abuse of sexual partners. Again if the light within us is darkness how can us Christians be a light to the world?

By contrast, the light of enduring and faithful love is a norm that arguably was never more needed. And it's one that meets both Christian and more universal aspirations. I have married many people in church. Always couples say to me, I found the one I was looking for, my soul mate and I know we are meant to be together forever. Hence the common phrase, he or she is searching for his or her soul mate, the other that completes the self. One can read it into the 2017 Oscar-winning film **La La Land**. It's a universal search and it is a universal aspiration; Christ's blessing is that he makes it more possible by his kingdom's redemptive power and his sacramental grace stemming from the sacrament of marriage within his holy church.

For what is unique in Christ's teaching here and what is really challenging for today is the insistence on suffering faithfulness, commitment no matter what, as the right relationship of the sexes according to God's plan. Again this is rooted in the perfection of older laws: "thou shalt not commit adultery", "thou shalt not covet thy neighbor's wife". But Christ goes beyond these in the Sermon. He gets to the heart of the problems involved in this area.

He boils it all down to the simple ideals that love should be real and true and sexual relations deeply rooted in lasting love. For anything less does not satisfy the human heart or endure. It can be just a destructive game of using the other for passing pleasure. If love is real, like God's love which scripture asks us to imitate, it is forever. Christ draws here on Genesis and the prophets, especially Hosea and his image of the relationship of God and his people as an indissoluble marriage:

> I will betroth you to myself forever betroth you with integrity and justice, with tenderness and love; I will betroth you to myself with faithfulness, and you will come to know your God.

This is the model for couples coming to really know and cherish each other in a life-long journey together. This excludes even adultery as a reason for breaking the marriage tie; Hosea took back his adulterous wife. Christ himself and his total love for us on the cross is the great model for this. Hence the church has traditionally seen the ideal of marriage faithfulness as an image of Christ's enduring love for his bride the church.

This suffering faithfulness may not be popular in the secular world today but it makes sense in communal Kingdom terms. The love commitment of the redeemed members of that community must be more than a superficial pretense, a passing mockery. They must cling to the true love's happiness and the oneness and faithfulness of the married commitment. That is also why same-sex marriage is not the ideal. Man and woman, created differently to complement each other in the unity of true love and marriage and to produce its fruits, is the Kingdom ideal. But where it fails there is compassion and forgiveness and non-judgmental healing.

For the Old Testament approach to human sexuality, which Christ is refining, is positive and two-fold in this respect too. In Genesis, creation's innate goodness, God's image in humankind and our thirst for fulfillment are all encapsulated in the male/female relation:

> It is not good for man to be alone...
> In his own image he created them,
>   male and female...and God saw that it was good.

There is also recognition of the fall in Genesis. Hence the ideal is restored in God's first covenant with his people. His vow of love, faithfulness and nurturing presence with his people is renewed in the redemption of the people on Sinai.

That redemptive vision is further echoed today in the sexual covenant of man and woman united in Christian marriage. This is part of the new Messianic covenant.

For purely erotic love hasn't the divine status in Genesis it's accorded in other Middle-Eastern cults. In Genesis, only faithful love between man and woman images the unconditioned and definitive acceptance of people in God's loving embrace. This sense of marriage as reflecting the covenant between God and his people is even more definitive when translated into the terms of Christ's redeemed Kingdom.

Yet in the Sermon there is both continuity and discontinuity with the Old Testament view. Marriage echoes the covenant love between God and humanity but is realized in a new definitive way in Christ. He is the bridegroom of God's new people and covenant. Jesus echoes Deuteronomy - "what God hath joined together let no man put asunder" - but he adds: "it was said to you in the past thou shall not commit adultery...but I say to you everyone who divorces his wife makes her an adulteress and whoever marries a divorced woman commits adultery".

Later revisions in Judaism of the original Old Testament Law allowed divorce. Christ restores the original intent. And he restates it in new prophetic messianic terms as it relates to the new Kingdom of God. The conduct of partners in Christian marriage in the early church, which Matthew reflects, is therefore measured by the love, faithfulness and self-giving of Christ for his church.

Moreover, it's not just love one another as you love yourself, but love one another as Christ loved us, total giving love. Paul in Ephesians calls this a "great mystery". The word mystery is translated in the Vulgate as "sacramentum". Here woman and man's love for each other is an epiphany of Christ's all-embracing love and faithfulness present in his church. This establishes the view of the eternal sacramental nature of marriage as it evolved in the church, which I will discuss in the next chapter.

CHAPTER 22

▼

The Fourth Antithesis and the Sacrament of Marriage

The sacramental nature of marriage formed the basis of Catholic thinking as it evolved. The word sacrament became explicitly linked to Christian marriage as Kingdom witness. But Old and New Testament perspectives, marriage as belonging to the order of creation and of redemption, divided Protestant and Catholic views at the reformation. Reformers such as Luther tending to lose sight of the second perspective, the prophetic "more" required and made possible in Christ's redeemed Kingdom, life-long Christian faithfulness in marriage as a sign of the Kingdom come. Vatican 11 explains:

> Authentic marital love is included in Divine Love and guided and enriched by the redeeming power of Christ, and the church's mediation of salvation.

The authentic love of husband and wife, moreover, is not just a symbol but a real sign of God's love fully expressed in Christ. More importantly, as Christ accepts the church as sinners so married people should accept each other again and again in all their dissatisfactions and with all their guilt, because human love and faithfulness are always completed by Christ's Easter victory. This "Kingdom come" redemptive dimension of marriage in Christ makes the Sermon's absolute demands in this area more understandable. It explains Christ's more radical stress on the blessedness of enduring love and faithfulness and the indissolubility of marriage. It is the redemption of the disintegration and fragmentalization of human sexuality, due to sin, that Christ also comes to heal within the Kingdom. Ideally, Christian married couples by their transcending love enter into the service of God and his new creation and redemption in Christ in this way.

So that God's love and faithfulness are made visible in a human way. This is another way to be "the light of the world", the "salt of the earth", to practice the "more" of the Kingdom. Happy marriage and family life are in a special sense the redeemed Kingdom in miniature, "the domestic church", as Vatican 11 says. Married couples have a special role in the building up of the Kingdom through their openness to children, example of faithfulness and as cells of community love, unity and hospitality.

Yet since good Christian marriage is the domestic church, it is not just a private but also a public affair. This is clear in the solemn way it's celebrated and the necessary presence of the priest. This communal dimension means that the church is answerable to God for the success of the marriage. The best word for marriage then is not contract but covenant. It's both public and private, a familial church covenant of love celebrated in public. And just as the covenant between God and his people is permanent, so is the new marriage covenant in Christ.

Neither the church nor marriage exist in themselves. They are eschatological signs of the gathering and reconciliation of mankind at the end of time and peace between nations that is the Kingdom ideal. Like the love within the Trinity, every child born of a loving union of two people, a world of happy united parents and children, that's God's dream and Christ's dream.

Christians who remain unmarried, priests, monks, and nuns who are celibate, live a similar life of loving commitment to the Lord and the Kingdom. They have as vital a role as married couples. Monks and nuns in other religions are publicly revered witnesses to the deepest aspects of the faith. Christian celibates for the sake of the Kingdom are similar. In this, Catholics maintain the celibate ideal for the sake of all the churches for full Christian imitation of Christ, the celibate lover of God and the Kingdom unto the cross and the resurrection.

Like faithful married couples, vowed Christian celibates affirm the role of the Christian as not flight from but redemptive service of the world. In the spirit of the beatitudes, their way of life is steadfast, gentle, merciful, idealistic, peaceful, poor in spirit, committed and faithful.

In marriage, suffering clinging to the vows made also entails persevering in love as a conscious choice after the first passion fades. It means staying true to vows made from a heart even when difficulties arise; clinging to the indissoluble nature of marriage through thick and thin.

Compromise undermines the inner idealism that brings true righteousness, erodes it bit by bit. So Christ opposes the "hardness of heart" of lawmakers in Israel who either allowed divorce in certain cases (the Pharisees) or liberally (the Sadducees). Christian idealism must be more than both. Though some churches allow divorce due to a later addition in Matthew, "except for adultery", most exegetes recognize that Christ did assert the absolute indissolubility of marriage. Indeed, anything other than this makes no sense in the context of Christ's general more radical "more" approach in the Sermon. It makes no sense for Christ to vehemently oppose the religious authorities who compromised the marriage ideal by allowing divorce and then in the next breath agree to compromise it himself. This also makes no sense in relation to his central injunction in The Sermon; "unless your righteousness exceeds that of the Scribes and the Pharisees, you cannot enter the kingdom of God". The Pharisees by allowing divorce in "hardness of heart" compromised the original law and that is precisely what Christ is trying to counteract in his new Kingdom by affirming even more strongly the Genesis injunction.

So Christ's vision of marriage in the Sermon is not transitory, a straw in every wind of passing fashion, it's an enduring code for all time, rooted in God's plan for the unity of the sexes. And it's rooted in a visionary restoring of the spirit of the old law. That's why Christ invokes Genesis in the Sermon. He is restoring the "purpose" of the law. It says that man and woman shall leave their parents and become one flesh. What God so unites no man or woman should divide; for this obstructs God's plan. His Kingdom people, his image restored in Christ, should do his will in this too with humble faithful hearts unto suffering righteousness.

Total Love, enduring commitment and faithfulness is the Kingdom ideal, imitative of the enduring and faithful love of God for us. He loves us warts and all to the end. This is how married couples should love each other. This ideal is the basis for enduring marriage and family life and is the way to true happiness. I often feel sorry for those actors and actresses who marry again and again. They pursue an empty illusion, never knowing the joy of loving someone warts and all, going with them through life to mature love in old age, producing the good wine at the last, and then entering into a final union for all eternity. For in the popular consciousness too there is that sense of the eternal nature of true love.

Where this is not possible, due to irretrievable breakdown in marriage, the other beatitude of suffering faithfulness should hold. Like Hosea's clinging to his unfaithful wife, we should honor the vows made no matter what. As the next antithesis shows, if we do not really mean the vows we make, then we shouldn't make them at all. So the marriage vows also dictate that we sacrifice a second chance; hence the "separation" teaching of the church. We remain true to what we vowed before God and others as a sacred trust though separated. We set kingdom faithfulness before our immediate desires. Indeed, Kasper thinks that even natural, or common law marriage, is part of this same mystery and has the same call to suffering faithfulness.

This may seem difficult today but the whole Sermon is about suffering in doing what's right, the state of the suffering just man who is vindicated in the long run for his meekness and who thereby helps to redeem the earth sunk in ruthless self-interest and more limited versions of love. Again Christ's new more radical command comes in here, "love one another as I have loved you". He loved us to the last drop of his blood on the cross. This links with the beatitudes. In gentle suffering and poverty of spirit we hold to marriage even unto the cross of faithful separation. When marriages fail the worldly tendency is to take the easy way out but suffering faithfulness is the Kingdom way for enduring marriage, home life and children's good.

A recent study showed that children who live in a separated or difficult relationship still do better than those whose parents have taken the way out of divorce. That is, messy divorces lead to endless problems for society and the children involved. Modern society's break-up of the family bears this out. Once the ideal goes, or is compromised, everything is permitted. The danger is that the ideal of the family and marriage itself may fall apart.

We might chart Christ's radicalism here too as the "more" of the Kingdom vision far above the old law's more limited one:

Chart 8

The old limited law	The unlimited new law
do not commit adultery	Be faithful
for basic social cohesion	for the new Kingdom
the law of Moses	the new love law of Christ
the old covenant	the new covenant in Christ's blood
for the old people of God	for the new people of God

This is a new way, but it is also one that has always been an ideal in human hearts. Indeed, the need for true and lasting love is still the "aspiration" of many today, in spite of the present liberal climate in relation to sexual mores in general. This is because it is rooted in the natural law. The need for love balance, for the enduring compatibility and complementarity of the sexes, is built into nature; a modern smash hit song puts it well: "when I fall in love it will be forever, or I'll never fall in love". At the human level, sexual relations to be fulfilling must be more than brute mating; there must be a spiritual and soul dimension, for man is a spiritual being. This again is universal. This is brought out well in that modern classic **The Karate Kid**. In it the old karate master says to his young male pupil, who is going for a date with the girl he loves: "life is all about balance…go find your balance". He is reflecting the eastern concept of yin and yang; that the key to all nature and human life is the union and balance of complementary opposites.

That great and very popular modern film **Sleepless in Seattle** makes the point well at the popular western cultural level. It shows the continuing relevance of Christ's love and marriage ideals today, their universal resonance. The heroine in the film has a sense of her one true love, the man who is her final destiny, without whom she will be incomplete, restless always, forever unhappy. She is temporarily prepared to marry someone she likes but doesn't love deeply, for security reasons. When he, her lukewarm lover, realizes this, and that she already has her destined soul-mate elsewhere, he hands her back the ring saying that marriage is too serious to be entered into from other than the highest motives. The film ends with the words of a beautiful Louis Armstrong song, "make someone happy, and you will be happy too".

This ideal of marriages made in heaven, another of Christ's Kingdom ideals, is then both new, and yet enshrined even in the non-Christian the world already. Indeed it is a pervasively present in popular culture. Our film industry practically lives off it. So do novelists, poets and love lyricists. Ninety per cent of our films, novels, plays and popular songs have this theme as central, "I will love you until I die". I think again of the words of Nat King Cole's famous song, "when I give my heart it will be completely, or I'll never give my heart". The song topped the charts for him, and topped the charts again in 1987 when recorded by Rick Ashley. It reflects the ideal that many, if not all, aspire to, and it is the ideal Christ offers us in the Sermon's teaching on sexuality and marriage.

The great example of such enduring love is Christ himself. He was not married, but he was faithful in love unto the cross. So he is the model for married people, and notably for celibate priests and religious (nuns receive a ring and are espoused to Christ at their final vows). Such a commitment is just as total and demanding a commitment as marriage faithfulness and just a vital for the church.

In this respect I think of that beautiful and much misunderstood book and film, **The Last Temptation of Christ.** It makes the point very well. Christ is tempted on the cross to come down, marry and have a family like everyone else and live as a carpenter, as a simple husband and father. In the film he does so in imagination. But years later, as he works at his lathe, the apostles come to him and say: "why did you let us down so badly". In effect, he had succumbed to the same temptation as Satan put to him in the desert, to put himself and his needs and desires before his mission of the cross, of being the faithful suffering servant of scripture. This was his marriage commitment as it were. And it was a similar self-giving to save the world, to be its light of love and unity. Christ on the cross is the supreme faithful lover unto the last drop of his blood. He experiences the clash of two great goods and timeless loves; that of marriage and family on the one hand, and that of the undivided love of God and humankind on the other, humankind's need for the saving cross of total giving love.

Even the apostles once wanted him to turn aside from that road and satisfy himself but after the resurrection they realize the wisdom of the cross. His faithfulness unto death is the great example for married couples who might be tempted to abandon their radical original commitment, and more so for consecrated religious.

This antithesis also anticipates how this ideal will come under attack from the evil one as Christ was attacked by Satan in the desert. But even in the film he does not come down and marry and have children, he does not betray his vows, any more that the married couple should; or any more than the celibate priest or religious should. For the latter's vows reflect and are as demanding a Kingdom form of faithfulness as those of Christ or the married couple. I often use this as an example for celibate priests and religious. For they too embrace the role of total commitment to the Kingdom, to suffering service of God and others, to the quest for perfection and holiness for the redemption of all beyond personal desire or gain.

There is also a beatitude dimension here of keeping and meaning the vows we make. That is another key reason why married couples should remain faithful through thick and thin. Keeping one's sacred vows, made before God and the community, is a prophetic imperative for being members of Christ's new Kingdom. Again this is reaffirmation of an ideal already present in the prophets and psalms. Take, for example, psalm 115:9-12:

My vows to the Lord I will fulfill, before all his people.
O precious in the eyes of the Lord is the death of his faithful.

This leads on the fourth antithesis. There is a logical progression in the antitheses. Marriage faithfulness, like the celibate or religious witness to the Kingdom, means also honoring one's vows unto death. But the one consolation in this, and throughout the Sermon, is the understanding also of human frailty, and the rich forgiving love of God for all who fail.

CHAPTER 23

The Fifth Antithesis: honoring one's Word

The fifth antithesis again embodies Christ's idealistic radicalism. The Sermon as a whole says compromise eats away, bit by bit, at the root of the moral heart. The fourth antithesis extends Christ's radicalism into the sphere of oral communication. This links with the Old Testament prophets again. Wisdom literature warned against frivolous oaths, and in the wider field of human discourse swearing false oaths or deliberate verbal ambiguity is seen as a dangerous thing, especially when these are used to justify all sorts of devious activities. This is condemned, for example, in **Ecclesiasticus** 23:12-14, which says false swearing brings the judgment of God on the miscreant:

> A man forever swearing is full of iniquity,
> And the scourge will not depart from his house.
> If he offends, his sin will be on him.
> If he swears lightly, he sins twice over;

> If he swears a false oath, he will not be treated as innocent, for his house will be full of calamities.

In the same vein, Jesus demands total trustworthiness in one's verbal relations with God and others, for the sake of human community. Only when all live in trust, true to and honoring their word come what may and free from verbal falsehood and related evils, can community unfold. This is a strong variation on the eight commandment of the Decalogue, which condemns swearing false oaths in court to incriminate one's neighbor.

This was regarded as very serious, like perjury is in the modern context; for it infringed both truth and could pervert the course of justice, even condemn the innocent. In the old law it was seen as punishable even by death; those who swore falsely against Daniel were thrown instead into the lion's den. Those who swore falsely against Susanna were punished just as severely. So Christ's antithesis is a refining variant on the old law here.

In this too Jesus is more radical and prophetic in style. He is moral liberator in relation to the law, for he goes much further than it in saying that one should not swear at all; this is how seriously he takes the breaking of vows or oaths. If we don't really mean them, or mean to live by them, they shouldn't be taken at all. As Meier notes, Christ finds any oath objectionable, because any kind of oath infringes on God's majesty and transcendence. Man is not to imagine that he can claim God as a witness, or control God for his own purposes (75).

This was taken up by James, a cousin of Christ's, who writing about thirty years after Christ's death echoes the Sermon, which suggests that it must have come directly from

Christ (Jas 5:12) (even the JBC says that the Epistle of James was probably an updating of a quite early tradition stemming from James of Jerusalem):

> Above all, my brothers, do not swear by the heaven or by the earth, or use any oaths at all. If you mean "yes" you must say "yes"; if you mean "no", say "no". Otherwise you make yourself liable to judgment.

With Christ this antithesis was addressed most of all to those, such as the Pharisees, who would use God to lend credence to their lies or evasions of the truth. He was all too aware of the clever sophistry of the religious authorities for corrupt ends. As the JBC notes:

> Jesus is here opposing the hypocrisy, sophistry, and academic trivialization of life and replacing them with the ideal of simplicity and directness of speech (643).

The inference is that our life or that of a community must not be a lie in any way even if it is a clever or white lie, but a constant witness to the truth of our verbal communications. This matches the radicalism of the rest of the Sermon. There must be no compromises with one's integrity of speech for that too can become a slippery slope leading to perdition.

When God is invoked in our false or devious vows they can become unforgivable blasphemy, "liable to the judgment" as James says. Moreover, Christ says, in an even stronger statement, that anything other than direct truthful speech "comes from the evil one".

In asking us to avoid oath-taking, he is saying that the truth of our verbal communications should not need an oath if one's words can truly be trusted. There is a subtle moral psychology underlying Christ's injunctions here. Those who need to invoke God are probably people whose words can't be trusted by others on their own merits anyway.

Christ says that our words should come from a pure heart, a heart rooted in truthfulness, so there should be no need for oaths. It is taken for granted that what we say comes from a pure and honest heart.

In the Catholic consciousness the opposite of this antithesis was seen mainly in terms of lying. It was one of the main sins we were asked to confess when I was young. It said that our society valued truthfulness. But this antithesis is about more than simple lying, it's about our trustworthiness with others in relation to our speech in every way, notably in keeping our promises, or fulfilling our boasts or honoring all verbal commitments. If we can't do that, we should not promise, or boast or make verbal commitments at all. I'm reminded of the code of the old Irish Fianna, the noble warrior race of the sagas in the Irish language: "gloine ar gcroi, is neart ar mhuini, is beart de reir ar mbriathar". The pagan Irish code might be straight out of the Sermon, proving again its universal validity. The slogan roughly translated says: purity of heart, strength of mind (bravery and consistency in virtue) and being true to one's word, promises, vows or boasts.

This sense of honoring one's word is a universal trait. In all the codes of honor, from chivalrous knights to Samurai warriors to Roman Senators, the sense of one's word as one's bond was sacred. Even in the old western films the ultimate challenge to draw was to tell someone that they were a liar. In medieval times, people even fell on their swords, or challenged others to a duel, if the honor of their word was impugned.

This sense of verbal integrity's importance is still strong today. In relation to the related keeping of our promises, or carrying out our undertaken responsibilities, one is reminded of Frost's poem **Stopping by Woods on a Snowy Evening**:

> The woods are lovely dark and deep,
> but I have promises to keep
> And miles to go before I sleep
> And miles to go before I sleep

The temptation is to take the easy way out, to sleep, to seek oblivion, but the poet is reminded that he has larger responsibilities that make it imperative for him to carry on. He has vows and promises to keep that cannot be ignored in favor of a suicidal or immoral escapism.

Again Christ is the model for keeping this antithesis. One of his great characteristic is his purity of Word and deed. No one, even his worst critics, could catch him out, or find anything derogatory in what he said. The trick of the Pharisees in relation to the paying of tribute to Caesar is a case in point. We are told that they were trying to catch him out in his speech so that they would have something to charge him with. His words, "render unto Caesar the things that are Caesar's and unto God the things that are God's", left them speechless. We are told they could find no fault in him and eventually stopped trying to catch him out in his speech altogether.

CHAPTER 24

▼

The Sixth Antithesis: Passive Resistance

In this antithesis Jesus returns to the problem of violence and war and puts forward the radical alternatives of passive resistance and total rejection of vengeance. Again there is logic here. This is a sure way to free the heart from what causes violence. Many modern figures and movements have shown the wisdom of such peaceful protest, from Daniel O'Connell in Ireland to Nelson Mandela in Africa. The underlying logic is that violence begets more violence. One must break that vicious cycle. A solution to conflict can be better achieved by quiet, persistent, peaceful and dignified opposition and the fruits of such a peace are usually more lasting.

Christ's vision in the Sermon goes further. One shouldn't return evil for evil in any circumstances. This calls to mind the Catholic precept that one should never try to achieve good ends by evil means. Using evil means undermines the good that is their end. Thereby one becomes as bad as the evil perpetrator, accelerating the evil process. One rather returns good for evil. This sense of turning the other cheek as the solution to violence inspired many modern pacifists to achieve their aims, as already mentioned. This gives the lie to those who say this does not work in practice or that it is too idealistic.

Moreover, this links with the other beatitudes. One can't solve violence by indulging in it oneself; one can't be poor in spirit, meek, merciful, conscious of what is right, or peaceful, if one hates and seeks revenge or wages endless war on enemies. The only way to solve world wars is to eschew violence, seek peaceful reconciliation.

One might say are we not required to fight against such as Hitler? But John Paul 11 in Poland or Gandhi in India showed that there is more than one way to defeat evil. Where there is no other way, the Catholic position is that there is such a thing as a just war but it must meet very strict conditions and be used only in very rare circumstances. In the context of modern weapons of mass destruction it's difficult to see how any major war between the great powers could meet the criteria for a just war.

The issue of Capital Punishment also arises here. Is it justified to execute a person who commits deliberate premeditated murder? Are we returning evil for evil in this? Obviously, the church and most modern countries who oppose Capital punishment think so.

The principal of non-violence at every level established by Christ is again rooted in the universal thirst for peace. It is the gentle, merciful, and compassionate values of the beatitudes. There is an internal coherence in these, deny one and you deny the whole; deny the heart focus in one, deny it in the other. I chart this as follows:

Chart 9

> Non-violence, turning the other cheek = being poor in spirit = being gentle = being peacemakers = being children of God.

Christ gives the lie to those who say he doesn't reason from basic principles. Everything in the Sermon stems, to a great extent, from the first beatitude, which is why it is the first. Just as the other commandments in the Decalogue stem largely from the first (most evils in the world stem from setting up false gods in opposition to the real one). Christ's Sermon teases out the logical implications of this creed of non-violence in other antitheses but its roots are in the Beatitudes, especially "blessed are the meek" and "blessed are the peacemakers".

Being faithful to the peaceful spirit and meekness of the earlier ways of blessedness, he not only tells us not to return evil for evil, but he spells out what this means in everyday terms: turning the other cheek, giving one's cloak to one who takes one's coat; going the extra mile; giving to all who ask; lending to all who borrow; not asking money back; and resolving legal disputes out of court to avoid any residue of bitterness. All this echoes the Psalms and Isaiah and their sense of the suffering servant whose reconciling meekness is a quality stemming from his surpassing goodness and gentleness rooted in God.

Why then hasn't this been the basis for Christian moral living in the west? Why do we constantly water down Christ's pacifist teaching? How in the so-called Christian west did we embark in our age on two terrible world wars? One explanation of course is that the ideologies behind those wars, from communism to fascism to imperialism, were militantly modern secularist rather than Christian.

In the film **Gandhi** when a western Christian advisor says to him that he should resort to violence to achieve Indian independence, Gandhi replies, "does not your Christ say to turn the other cheek". "Ah", the advisor replies, "we don't take that literally". In effect, due to his correspondence with Tolstoy, Gandhi was a better Christian than his so-called Christian advisor. And when a war broke out between India and Pakistan after independence, Gandhi fasted until they stopped fighting; another gentle peaceful way of resolving the conflict.

So why do we in the so-called Christian west apologize for Christ's obviously workable response to war, while at the same time trying to blame our religion for war (anyone with even half a brain can see that the terrible world wars of our era had nothing to do with religion; and the ideologies behind the Holocaust, the gulags, the purges, and the Killing Fields were profoundly anti-religious). Why did we pursue imperialist, fascist or communist models that caused world wars in opposition to Christian teaching? I think the reason is because Christ's peace way is too demanding; it nullifies our power lust. Is that also the reason why we turned, and continue to turn from it to secular totalitarian ideologies? Is it because we want war systems that justify our will to dominate others by force in the interest of world domination or a thirst to control the world's sources of wealth? Is Christ's way is too profound, too demanding, and imposes too many restraints on our darker desires in what was and is, arguably, a war-like libertine secular age? These are questions we must ask in the interests of learning from our western mistakes and finding another way forward.

The Sermon's pacifist way is pure liberation in this respect. Sure it may seem over idealistic, but surely the best moral codes must set the highest standards. What's the use in tuning our faith or morality to the reductionist morals of the world rather than God's ideal way of joyful, blessed and peaceful living? Why ignore his perfect peaceful moral vision for one of war mongering?

For this antithesis is not just an ideal, it works. This is illustrated in John Paul 11's toppling of totalitarian tyranny in Europe. During the Nazi suppression of the church, Jews, and the whole Polish nation, an adviser asked him to resort to violence. "No", he said, "we will conquer by love". He did so. He overcame the subsequent communist repression in the same way, helping to destroy the "iron curtain" in Europe. The peaceful toppling of the Berlin wall is another example. So is the organized peaceful resistance of the Solidarity Movement which brought down the communist system in the Soviet Union. All these instances prove how powerful the peaceful way is. Also John Paul 11 did not seek revenge against the man who shot him, but embraced and forgave him in prison. Everyone applauded this; which shows we appreciate and want this way deep down. The Sermon is a universal way to moral harmony, one which the best have lived and proved in our age. Christ's truth here is beautiful, and when lived brings beauty and peace to every aspect to life.

This was also proved in action in the peaceful civil rights movement in the USA in the Sixties, in cultural heroes like Luther King, and Joan Baez with her "We Shall Overcome" slogan (she also went to Sarajevo during the Balkan war with the same message). They embodied and showed the relevance of this antithesis for today. In peaceful words and actions they worked for African American rights and against the Vietnamese war draft and showed how much better the peaceful way is. It works better than violence and leaves no residue of bitterness. This was proved also by the peaceful civil rights marches in Northern Ireland, until that movement was high jacked by violent men who gave us the Troubles.

Christ is the supreme example of the eschewing of the violent way as he prayed for his enemies on the cross. He echoed the Old Testament prophecies which see the just man offer his back to those who would strike him, and his face to those who would pluck out his beard. He is the just man who bears all evils for God's sake, who lives his life in integrity and peace, despite the efforts of the wicked to pervert his peaceful heart into violence. He is Christ before Pilate, refusing to answer or defend himself against the wicked accusers, conscious that to do so is to compromise his vision of the meek, gentle and suffering servant of God. He not only preached but lived what he had preached in the Sermon by turning the other cheek at his trial. And, curiously, he is really the one in charge before Pilate, living out of his choice in the desert to be the suffering servant of God and others, rather than the violent ruler of all the kingdoms of the world, as represented to him by Satan as a key temptation. This choice links naturally with the next antithesis.

CHAPTER 25

▼

The Seventh Antithesis: Loving One's Enemies

Like the beatitudes, the antitheses follow logically. After telling us to turn the other cheek and reject war and revenge, the seventh antithesis takes this approach another logical step, that of loving even one's enemies: "it was said to you in the past you must hate your enemies but I say to you love your enemies, do good to those who hate you, pray for those who persecute and calumniate you". This is especially unique to Jesus, as Keretszty notes:

> The commandment to love one's enemies is acknowledged as unique to Jesus even by those interpreters who attempt to show that Jesus can be understood simply as one of many Jewish rabbis and charismatic healers (400).

Again the object is inner peace, and to ensure that that peace will become the norm in society. That is impossible if everyone carries on endless wars with "enemies", real or imagined, and seeks revenge for every real or imagined wrong. Peace is impossible, endless violence is inevitable, if everyone seeks to achieve his or her desires for power, wealth, domination and vindication by force, and by constantly creating enemies to fight against for glory. This aspect is fleshed out by James, who echoes the Sermon, in his early letter to the budding churches (Jas 4:2-3):

> Where do all the fights and quarrels among you come from - you want things and you cannot have them, so you are prepared to kill.

There is consistency here with the earlier beatitudes. If we are poor in spirit we do not seek to enforce our desires by force, desires for wealth, power, pleasure or fame, or our prideful and arrogant thirst for revenge. These desires cause much violence in the world. If we're to make a difference, we must break the cycle that endless war with our enemies entails.

But this antithesis is more than the negative injunction of avoiding trouble; it is a strong positive command. We must actively love our enemies: try to be extra nice to them, win them over with a gentle approach. It requires strength to do that, the way of hate and violence is easier. Yet only the reconciling approach of the gentle man brings peace; showing "enemies" we can be friends, burying the hatchet in every way.

In the light of the whole Sermon this demand is very logical. It fits with the Sermon's vision of morality as rooted in godly goodness and Kingdom fellowship. Jesus teaches filial imitation of God who pours his sunshine on sinners and saints alike. His morality, his heart of love even towards those who hate him, must become human morality if the world's evils are to be solved.

There is another element distinguishing the Christian from pagan counterparts, and it accounts for the sermon's radicalism. Kingdom morality imitates Christ, who in imitation of his Father is an example of unconditional love on the cross. So loving enemies, foolish in worldly terms, mirrors God's all-encompassing love for us, even while we are hopeless sinners. As Kereszty notes:

> Loving one's enemy becomes the most characteristic attitude of the one who undergoes metanoia (a complete change of heart). Only by loving his enemy does he "prove" that he has understood and accepted God's love for himself, who, as a sinner, had been God's enemy (85).

Indeed, as Von Balthasar says, this is how we discover our true identity. The Sermon on the Mount shows man created from the beginning in the image of God. Jesus takes up this image and directs it beyond itself to the prototype:

> Christ becomes the only interpreter of God, but by the same stroke the interpreter of man. By letting the light of the prototype fall upon the image, he gives man his dignity and truth (283).

Moreover, this is given an eschatological dimension in Christ's vision. Final peace with God, ourselves, others, and nature is our eternal destiny, a state of **shalom,** the state of the just man of the Old Testament who remains true to God and at peace with himself and others even in the face of fierce attack and persecution by his enemies. It is the sure prerequisite for eternal peace for we cannot go before God and into eternity with hating hearts; we may be so for all eternity.

Indeed, this eschatological dimension is filled out further when Christ says if we love only our friends what merit is there in that. So this is a special Kingdom way that earns extra merit for us in the eschatological end time.

That is, to be with God forever we must be more like him here. Hence the final injunction of the Sermon: "be you perfect as your heavenly Father is perfect". This is the Ten Commandments and the Sermon in a nutshell. Loving our enemies belongs to the same perfection as God practices, and it is our birthright as his sons and daughters in Christ.

But is it relevant today? Perhaps the great example of this beatitude in action is Shakespeare's **Romeo and Juliet**. In that play two feuding families are brought together by tragic love. They learn thereby the futility of their perpetual hating of supposed enemies. Shakespeare may have had the Sermon in mind. Certainly, the uselessness of the whole concept of "enemies" is expressed, the stupidity of hate for anyone for whatever specious or invented reason. The deliberate keeping of hate alive is even more senseless. For all, once we get to know them, are eminently lovable. If we make the effort to know and love them we will be rewarded by much returned love. This is the logic of Christ's position.

The point is also made in that beautiful modern book and film, **The Boy in the Striped Pyjamas**. Bruno, the child of a concentration camp commander befriends a Jewish boy, Shimon, who is a camp inmate. Bruno, by befriending the little Jewish inmate of the nearby concentration camp run by his father, rejects in action what he is told by Nazi propagandists, that all Jews are enemies of the German state. Every day the two young boys sit and play together, one outside the barbed wire and one inside it; and Shimon eats the food Bruno brings him. They become the best of friends. But one day a guard finds Shimon eating the food and accuses him of stealing it; he replies that Bruno had given it to him. But when the guard asks Bruno, out of fear he says: "no, I didn't give it to him".

Later, he finds the little Jewish boy all beaten up as a result and he is says "can you forgive me I don't know why I did it!" Shimon does so but he is hurt by the betrayal of his friend. Then he begins to cry, his father is missing and no one can find him. The German boy says, "I will come into the camp and help you find him, just give me a pair of the striped pyjamas you wear". The father has been gassed, and while the two children look for him, they too are rounded up with the others and taken to the gas chamber. They die together holding hands, the innocent Jewish and German boy, innocent victims of a hating world they can't understand. Which shows again the universal nature of the sermon's injunction to love one's enemies; at heart, as innocent young people, we tend to accept everyone. The film is very much of the Sermon, for the two boys in their natural state and consciences don't see each other as enemies. The whole cult of hate imposed on them by old men, cold secular ideologues, makes no sense. They just naturally love each other as equal human beings.

Again Christ is the model in this innocent loving of all God's children. His love for his enemies is echoed in everything he does. It is seen in his refusal to condemn those who condemned him. Even before Herod, who had conspired against his life, he allows himself to be treated like a fool. And before Pilate he scarcely defends himself, though the latter had the power to sentence him or set him free. He does not condone the sin of those who condemn him, but he does not bear a grudge against anyone, even on the cross.

Indeed, the main sign of his love for his enemies is his prayer for those who are crucifying him. On the cross, he says of the religious leaders who demanded his life because he tried to win them over to the true way of God, the father of all: "Father forgive them they know not what they do".

This suffering gentleness of Christ is the embodiment of the antithesis he preached here. Even those who hardened their hearts against his saving love he wept over and wanted to gather as a hen gathered her chickens under her wings. It's the attitude also of the other prophets who went before him (he is the last and greatest of the prophets as the Son of God). The prophets also forgave their persecutors, and did so out of love, and also to try to wean them from the way of hatred and spiritual destruction to the gentle way of God.

CHAPTER 26

Spiritual bases and reasons for the way of the Beatitudes

These later parts of the sermon outline the vital spiritual bases needed to underlie all that went before, for without spiritual bases in the heart all law or injunction is in vain. That is, the Sermon's morality is made possible, as all morality should be, by a deep related spirituality. Indeed, that is the key role the church plays in society; the nourishment of our immortal souls, for all else is passing and dust and ashes in the long run, and our souls need to be nourished even more than our bodies; governments are foolish to ignore that aspect without which the development and all-round health of society is bound to be impaired, and society will be a failure; man is also a spiritual being and his or her souls need to be nourished too, for their deeper all-round happiness, that of the inner man and woman.

The spirituality of the Sermon enables us to put the horse of inner spirituality before the cart of morality, so that it will carry us all the way down the road, to happiness here and hereafter. For above all, for our perfection, we need the help of God's guidance and grace. We can't do it on our own. We need to be redeemed. Can anyone looking at Auschwitz say we don't need to be redeemed? True morality, and the resultant good and peace of humankind, can only grow out of true spirituality - prayer of the heart, personal fasting, alms giving, all the key inner aids to moral perfection that are also for the total good of society. Again this is a universal perception. It's seen also, for example, in the Buddhist monk entering the monastery, and placing himself in the hands of a master who can show him the way to enlightenment. The Christian master of course is Christ, who shows us the spiritual pillars on which all houses of morality stand, enabling all to stand erect by his grace.

Again this is both Christian and universal. His foregrounding of prayer, fasting and alms giving, as key spiritual paths to perfection, are also basics of other world religious spiritual systems orientated towards the good. They are for example also the pillars of Islam: prayer five times a day to link us with God; fasting to purify the heart (fasting makes prayer a thousand times more effective), and alms giving to free us from the tyranny of greed. Hence the special time of prayer and fasting and alms giving in Islam, the forty days of Ramadan.

Christians, in a similar way but for different reasons, purify their hearts to celebrate the major events of the faith, notably Christmas and Easter, by prayer, fasting and alms giving. But we do so for different reasons. These spiritual paths are all orientated towards, or should be orientated towards, Christ's Kingdom come to redeem the world. They are imitative of his continuous prayer apart, his fasting in preparation for his public ministry, and his continual giving of himself in works of healing and charity during his public ministry. Even Christ, though perfect, saw the need for spiritual aids. He often prayed apart, and this energized his preaching and the active charity of his public ministry. So let's examine these key spiritual bases in detail.

(1) Authentic Alms giving

Alms giving are one of the key spiritual ways Christ outlines to enable us to gain purity of heart. It is again linked to both the beatitudes and the Old Testament, especially the psalms, which sum up some of the key attributes of the just man as:

> Open hearted he gives to the poor.
> He is generous, merciful and just.

Charity was well organized in Judaism and given a high status. But for Jesus alms giving is associated with the great virtues of mercy, gentleness and justice. We give to rid ourselves of greed, to purify the heart, and to make us people of peace and love for all, notably the poor.

The key aspect here, however, is not showy charity, but giving from a pure and generous heart, without calling attention to oneself. Again the heart is central. We must not do it to please men, but from the heart to please God; "let your light shine before men that seeing your good works they may give glory to your Father in heaven". So purity of intention and act is what all charity must come from to be real. There is no divine reward for charity unless it is pure humble giving.

Again Jesus drives this lesson home with the key literary device of paradox, our right hand must not know what our left hand is doing. What a neat and humorous phrase. It's

Jesus the poet or the clown as he was often depicted in medieval literature. We give alms for Jesus and for the Kingdom, for a heavenly not an earthly reward. And we give alms in a totally unassuming way. Again, poor in spirit, our mercy is not orientated towards ourselves or for self-gratification - am I not great in doing this - but humbly done for love of God and the good of the needy other.

(2) Authentic Prayer of the heart

Like authentic charity, true prayer from the heart is the next great pillar of virtue. It is one key source by which we get the grace that makes virtue possible, for faith is not an ideology or partial like the ideologues of the world that demonize all opposing ideologues (these usually begin as revolutions and end as tyrannies; free speech is allowed only if its "liberal" or "Marxist" or "conservative" or whatever; for example, dare one oppose the political correctness mores of the present liberal ideology in the west?). But faith is not an ideology, though people constantly try to make it such, hence the various persecutions of the church when it refuses to do so. Christian faith is a growing *relationship* with God in Christ within the bosom of the church, a relationship with eternal wisdom; which is why faith can't really be learned or reduced to knowledge it can only be experience within a *faith community*. The church has rolled on past thousands of opposing and ultimately passing purely man-made ideologies, because it is based on a communal relationship with God in Christ that raises us up to heavenly wisdom and glory and fully satisfies our vital spiritual needs within.

For this we need prayer. As any relationship is furthered by talk and communion with the loved one, so union with

God comes through prayer, the Word and the Eucharist. And prayer must not be self but God orientated, and not always about endless petitioning. As the JBC says:

> The positive teaching (of Christ) is that prayer should be sincere personal communion with God and that it should be brief because it is for our good, not God's, since he already knows what we need (644).

This is imitating Jesus in the Gospels where we are told he frequently went to apart to a quiet place to pray. It was out of that prayer that his ministry flourished, and the inference is that it must be the same for his disciples.

This is also part of the righteousness that exceeds that of the scribes and Pharisees, whose prayer was hypocritical. They loved to say prayers standing up in the synagogues and at street corners for people to see. The private prayers of the Jews had set times and formulas, but as Meier notes:

> Some would make sure they were in the synagogues or on the street corners when the set times came, so that they would have an audience (58)

By contrast Christ says that personal private prayer, real communion with God alone, is the ideal one should seek. It alone brings great blessings and rewards from God. Yet it is also seen in the man pure in heart who stands in the holy place or the righteous priest within the inner sanctum who worships the Lord on behalf of the community, as in psalm 24:

> Who shall ascend the mountain of the Lord,
> and stand in his holy place,
> he who has clean hands and a pure heart
> who desires not worthless things.

Though Christ commends private prayer in the secrecy of one's room, we cannot thereby infer that he was against community prayer. He himself participated in the synagogue worship and his great Eucharistic prayer at the Last Supper was a communion with his apostles as well as God. The point is that prayer must be aimed at God alone, so that God may give its rewards. True prayer is an encounter with God where we enter into his very life within our core, in community or alone; indeed, in that sense the greatest communion is the public Eucharistic one.

Above all, Christ sets Christian prayer apart from that of the pagans, who think that the more they babble the more likely it will be that their gods will hear them. Whereas the real God already knows what we need since he knows and sees all things and has providential care of us. Yet the prayer of petition is not redundant. We pray so as to commune with God, but also to ask for things we need, because of our freedom God can't force anything on us. He cannot give us good things, even heaven, unless we ask.

There is an insight here also into the nature of God, especially when Christ gives the prayer that is at the center of the Sermon, the Our Father. It's the perfect personal and communal prayer. Again there is a logical progression here. Christ talks about authentic prayer and then gives us the perfect example, a succinct summary of the whole Sermon, a succinct summary of the whole nature and trust of personal and communal prayer within the Kingdom community. Tertullian describes the Our Father as a perfect summary of the Gospel. Certainly, it is the perfect Kingdom prayer, and this is why it's given at the Sermon's center.

CHAPTER 27

▼

The Our Father, the perfect prayer of the Kingdom

The Our Father says everything we need to say as Christians; that's why Christ only gave us this prayer. It also gives us the perfect image of God, the center of all goodness. Christ describes God as not a remote pagan deity whose anger we must assuage, but as a loving Father, close to his children, feeling their needs. We should talk to him in prayer as a child would talk naturally to his dad, to Abba (daddy), as Luke says, in loving trust.

Matthew, very much the evangelist of the early church, adds a communal dimension to the prayer intimacy between God and us. Meier says: "we experience God's fatherhood not as isolated individuals but as members of the church" (60). This is proved by the fact that the petition is to "our" Father, as distinct from Jesus's "my" Father, though without any sense of difference in the relationship.

God's communal fatherhood includes each individual and his children everywhere. And, the JBC says, the Our

Father suggests that at the communal, individual and universal level the true relationship with God is one of "childlike trust, intimacy and readiness of access" (645). This is the characteristic sense of God in the New Testament (Rom 5:2, Eph2:18, 3:12, Heb10:17-20). But it is also there in parts of the old dispensation. This prayer must have grown out of Jesus's own worship. One also finds in the prophets, and in the psalms, the sense of a God who is infinitely close to his people, whom we praise from our inner being, e.g. psalm103:

> Bless the Lord, O my soul;
> And all that is within me bless his holy name!
> Bless the Lord, 0 my soul,

This also highlights another key purpose of prayer, to praise God, or hallow his name. This prayer reflects the spirit of the Beatitudes in which we're not only to imitate and revere Jesus, but also the gentle Father he mirrors. The image of Jesus as meek and mild and the Father as somehow more remote is bad theology, the two are one.

So this is the Kingdom prayer of the Father as well to the Father. It centers on seeing God as a gentle loving Father in heaven. This relates to the ideal of being poor in spirit but now it's God who is seen as such. It shows God as gentle, meek and humble in his relationship with us too.

We tend to see Jesus as coming from God, but we don't always see the Father as the reflection of Jesus, and their unity in the Spirit. So if Jesus is the suffering servant of humanity so is the Father. He suffers like Jesus until our greater good and happiness is achieved, like a true father suffers for his children's good.

Moreover, this prayer by showing God as a good Father ensures that our prayers, orientated towards the coming of the Kingdom, will be answered. This is infinitely consoling, for we not only see this Father as the fount from which all our ideals flow, but also the means by which we can make them into a reality in the world. This also gives a non-egotistic purpose to our spreading of Kingdom's righteousness, to hallow or glorify our Father in heaven. Bathed in his love, we want others to be similarly blessed, and he enables us to do so.

This was Jesus's mission. The Father is in heaven, but the Son on earth fulfills his will that all humankind should come to the fullness of his saving love. The prayer tells us that we're all so raised to heaven, able to call God Father and pray to him with complete trust.

So "hallowed be thy name", follows naturally. It expands on the Old Testament image of God, where the hallowing of his name is associated with recognition of his majesty, or holiness, in the midst of his beloved people (Ez36:23, Isaiah's oft repeated "the Holy One of Israel"). There he is also a father: "for I am a father to Israel, Ephraim is my first-born son" (Jr31:7-9). He is a mother too in Hosea, a boon for feminists. God's love for his people is shown in terms of the tenderness of a mother towards a child; like one who holds a child to her cheek and dangles him on her knee and leads him with leading strings of love (11:4-5).

As the new people of God in Christ we bask even more in that tender fatherly/motherly care. And we seek for others the universal blessing of his holy name and the coming of his Kingdom in Christ. Indeed Meier translates the phrase "hallowed be thy name" as: "sanctify your name by bringing in your Kingdom, the final day of all people's great liberation" (61).

"Thy Kingdom come" follows naturally. It is both a present reality for the baptized, and a future hope for all. It has come in Christ and is present in our communion with God as father in prayer, but it is still partial in the world at large. As Paul says it is like a woman straining in pain until birth, then the pain becomes joy. We pray constantly until our Father's Kingdom is complete, that we will be able to bring it about with his help for God can't give us anything unless we ask, because of our essential freedom.

In this, the Our Father highlights above all the mysterious centrality of prayer in Christian life. We have to pray as well as work for God's kingdom come. Indeed fervent prayer is one of our main vocations. Without it the kingdom cannot and will not come. Otherwise Jesus wouldn't ask us to pray urgently for its coming. The whole area of worship then is highlighted in the Sermon, as making possible the Kingdom values it charts.

By putting this prayer right at the center of the Sermon, Christ says that the kingdom can only grow through a powerful on-going relationship with the Father through prayer. God can't do anything unless we ask, even save the world. So prayer is not just about our humility before our loving Father, it's about that Father's humility before us.

Asking us to pray for the coming of the Kingdom on earth, Jesus infers that it cannot be unless we pray it into being, an extraordinary inference. How is this possible? It's because of human freedom. God cannot force anything, not even salvation on us or the world we must want and pray for it with all our hearts. He can bring it about only by our co-operation. This is logically in keeping with the gentle God of the beatitudes who forces nothing on us.

The Our Father might be called the Kingdom Prayer and the Sermon the Kingdom morality. Both are intimately related. Once the proper foundations of prayer are in place, heaven on earth will be furthered gradually, until God's will can be done "on earth as it is in heaven". As God is, as Christ is, so shall the Kingdom be. Let me chart this:

Chart 10

> God's kingdom come = equals God's will on earth as it is in heaven = the morality of the Son in practice = a world of humble service and justice = gentleness of life = lifting up of those who mourn = a world where thirsting for what is right is satisfied = a merciful compassionate world = a world where all are pure in heart = a peaceful world = those persecuted for right raised up = all being the salt of the earth and the light of the world = the fulfillment of the old law = new perfect standards in relation to avoiding violence = healthy sexual relations = enduring love between the sexes = indissolubility of marriage = keeping our word = returning good for evil = loving even one's enemies = indiscriminate and pure charity = authentic sincere prayer = God as our Father = his kingdom come.

It's about doing his will for our happiness that we pray into being.

CHAPTER 28

Thy will be done On Earth as it is in Heaven

All the Our Father petitions hinge on self-giving rather than self-seeking. So the third petition of the Our Father echoes Jesus's prayer in Gethsemane, "not my will but thine be done". The Father is in heaven but we pray for his will to be done on earth, for what Christ came to fulfill, his plan for our redemptive happiness here and hereafter.

But why is prayer so necessary for this? If God is all powerful why does he need our prayer? You would think that God could do it without us or our prayers! But the extraordinary paradox here again is that the will of God can only be done through our wanting it deeply, and that motivation can only come from communion with him in prayer. There is a circular literary logic here. The Kingdom cannot come unless we want it with all our hearts and we won't want it unless we pray for it and God can't give it until we want it. He can't bring it about in a vacuum of our will. Humanity's will must accord with God's will before a just world can come. He can do nothing against our will.

Applying this to our era; this explains why God was helpless before Hitler or Stalin. God cannot interfere even with our freedom to do evil. All hinges on our freedom, even suffering. If God solved all problems of sickness etc., we'd be manipulated puppets without freedom of will or being, which no one wants; we'd be mindless puppets as it were of a manipulative Sugar Daddy God. So good or evil in the world hinges on our right exercise of our free will.

This is the answer to those who say, why does God allow suffering? Why does he allow world cataclysms, or allow cancer to proceed in us and do nothing? If he interfered to solve everything, then we would be just puppets, our freedom, our most precious gift from him, would be out the window. He chooses not to be an all-controlling tyrant. Even the natural world must take its free course, with all the diseases and suffering and imperfections that came with the fall. But though God does not normally interfere in the world's free functioning this does not mean that he does not feel with and suffer for us as Jesus did. In Christ's Kingdom he shows us how, and gives us the grace needed, to redeem all that. But that can only happen with the co-operation of our free will as his free children.

In heaven the angels and saints do his will out of love not compulsion. We pray for the same on earth. For people even choose, rather than are given heaven or hell at death. It's never God's choice that anyone is lost. God's will is done in heaven, but remains to be done by his children on earth. This involves even their choice be saved or not.

All morality and prayer is not about God's dominance but our ultimate good and that of the world we live in. It's about his will being done for a redeemed Kingdom community that eventually, helped by our prayers, will spread to heal the whole world. For its true happiness that God wants for us, not for himself. But his raising of us to heaven, restoring the original creation, is achieved only by our co-operation and prayer. That's a logical conclusion we reach studying the Our Father. The paradox is that he needs our co-operation, because of our other tendency to perverse irreligious will, to bring us to the happiness here and hereafter that is our true destiny.

So the Our Father is as much about the humility of God as our humility. Our poverty of spirit, our need for him, is matched by his need for us and our prayer because of his love (though God actually needs nothing he chooses to need us). Otherwise, why would Christ ask us to pray constantly for the coming of God's Kingdom for our benefit? Prayer has a key role in the world. World and church happiness hinges on the eschatological completion of God's plan in Christ. That in turn hinges on the mystery of our will and God's becoming one through prayer.

This is given a practical application in the next phrase of the Our Father: "give us this day our daily bread". We can't even gain our basic needs without praying for them, or rather if we pray for them we're surer to get them. Scholars see this as related to the justice of the earlier beatitudes, feeding the hungry, clothing the naked, which Christ sees elsewhere as the main way we gain our reward at his Second Coming. He, like the Father, identifies with the poor and oppressed. "I was hungry and you gave me to eat", he will say, on the last day, to those who helped the poor. The Father, one with Christ, suffers with the poor because they are his children; another amazing truth.

This is not up in the air or empty faith it's about praying for and actively willing salvation for all in the here and now. We implore the Father to give us our everyday material needs for he cannot give them unless we ask and work for them. Again his humility respects our freedom.

Bread was the staple food of Christ's day, especially for the poor; we pray here for basic needs. We must pray for and help "feed the world", as the Band Aid song says in a modern context. People everywhere, even pop stars, can identify with this prayer's active benevolent aims.

Liberation theologians also take much comfort from the Our Father. God is not indifferent to our material needs; their achievement worldwide is also achieved by our Kingdom prayers and our actions as free children acting in tandem with his grace, love and power.

Inherent in this prayer also is our need to pray for the "daily bread" of the Eucharist, a reminder that the lifting up of the world also entails catering for people's deeper spiritual welfare, the salvation they need even more than life. We pray to ensure that their crying out for God, and his saving presence and love, is answered too. People persistently cry for deliverance from darkness of every kind, from death, guilt and inner pain. This "mourning" lot of man is only permanently and fully comforted by the access to God. We pray that all will accept his healing available to all in Christ. For people can reject that too, like a child who rejects his father's outstretched arms. Our returned love must be freely willed. That's why Christ had to come on earth and die on the cross, to convince us of God's saving love for us and persuade us to accept it freely. Prayer creates the inner dispositions for us to do so. It puts us closely in touch with the Lord who raises us up to our true dignity as his beloved children, and makes us in the church a conduit for his overflowing grace.

The need for a deeper spiritual mode of life that leads to a deeper happiness here and hereafter is why every culture has its monks, priests, nuns, Temples and deep wisdom scriptures. As Jesus says to Satan, "man does not live on bread alone". This links with the ultimate covenant relationship with God in Christ's body, the "bread of life" of the Eucharist. We pray for the bread of life, for God's fullness with us in Christ to lead us freely on the way to inner happiness. That's why Christ describes himself as the bread come down from heaven. He is the totally satisfying food that feeds us in every way during our journey through the sometimes barren desert of life, as God fed his people, the Israelites, in the desert, in their journey from slavery to freedom in the land flowing with milk and honey. Hence Christ says we cannot have "life in us", unless we eat this vital bread of the Kingdom, as part of a communal unity with him that overflows to vitiate the world with goodness.

Even the perfect way of moral righteousness spelled out in the Sermon can only come to full fruition in a truly spiritual heart, fed with the bread of God's Word, and the living bread of his presence with us in the Eucharist. So in the Lord's Prayer we also pray for this bread and it's completion in the final banquet of eternal life, of which it is a real foretaste.

What we pray for also in this supreme prayer is for that equally essential gift of God, his healing forgiveness: "forgive us our trespasses, as we forgive those who trespass against us". Again this is about our inner need for God's mercy. And it is only viable if we're merciful ourselves. And God's forgiveness is only possible if we're humble enough to ask for it and accept it freely. That's why, again, without prayer for forgiveness we can't attain it; God can't and won't force it on us. He cherishes and respects our freedom. Because we're fallen and sinful, yet racked by desire for what's right, we can only progress in holiness if we have his forgiveness; otherwise our guilt will become a weight on our shoulders that we cannot alleviate, and at death we may sink like a stone into the underworld. Hence the Sacrament of Reconciliation is another great gift.

Though we sorely need God's forgiveness in confession, for inner freedom here, and our eternal soaring in the sinless heavens, before we can attain it we must forgive others their "debts", for we can't expect mercy from God if we are merciless ourselves. Debts were a euphemism for sins in scripture. The forgiving hole has to be within our own souls, as it were, before God can fill it up. Even psychologists agree. As regards criminals, for example, they say that the latter must show real remorse, and seek real forgiveness from those they hurt, before they can make progress towards a new life and rehabilitation.

A similar law applies to victims. Psychologists say, victims must seek justice yes, but also reach a stage where they can truly forgive those that hurt them, otherwise they may carry an ever-increasing burden of resentment through life and on into the grave and no one wants to dwell in the darkness of a hating heart for all eternity. Moreover, forgiveness, the Lord's Prayer says, is vital for society also, lest grievances mount to the point where violence is inevitable. Peaceful societies are those most open to, and most availing of various forms of communal forgiveness.

That is, forgiveness is part of a wider liberation we pray for in the Our Father, the total liberation from evil, the most enslaving power of all. That is why the final phrase of the

Our Father centers on the summary of Christ's mission. He came to deliver us from the evil and darkness that has tormented the world, and is in each human being since the fall. I am amazed that some slur over this phrase, "deliver us from evil", when saying the Our Father. This phrase is the summary of the whole prayer, and indeed the whole of our faith. That faith is all about our free choice to be saved from evil, to enter freely into the salvation offered us by Christ our Lord. The Father's achieved total liberation for us in Christ, for this world's happiness and the next, but he needs our prayer and real co-operation in ensuring all accept that freedom.

That is why the question of temptation also enters in here. How can we resist the perennial temptation to evil within ourselves and in the wider world without the help of Our Father and his Christ? For the central temptation we all face is that faced by Christ in the desert, to pursue our own short-sighted kingdom of power, wealth, glory and even evil, over the bones of God and fellow human beings. This is the negation of all the beatitudes. It's the refusal to be poor in spirit, to recognize those who mourn as a result, to be merciful and just, even at the expense of our own ambitions, to be the suffering servant of God and others even unto death like Christ. That is, we need to move from the negativity of our evil tendencies and acts into the positive freedom of the children of God.

In effect, resisting temptation is not about something good that we have to reject in obedience to a policeman God, as it is often perceived (hence the joke, the best way of dealing with temptations is to give in to them). Resisting temptation is about choosing the way of happiness rather than accepting soul destruction and death. It is seeing through the illusions that the evil one puts before us to lure us away from free choice of God and what's right, illusions that destroy us in body and soul here so that even when we die and come to face eternity we will choose hell too. It's no joking matter it's a matter of our happiness here and hereafter that's at stake. Lead us not into temptation we cry lest we be lured down the evil road bit by bit, sin by sin, to the realm of damnation where there is weeping and gnashing of teeth forever.

Scripture describes this false attraction of evil beautifully, using the metaphor of eating. Evil ways seem sweet at first but when eaten they turn sour in the stomach and infect the whole person. By contrast, goodness often seems sour to taste at first but eventually it turns to pure sweetness in the stomach enriching the whole body. That is, our soul becomes sweetness and light by means of good acts and thereby we radiate that light to all around us.

The Lord's Prayer says that the power of prayer is needed here too. We must ask God's help in prayer to be able to resist the temptation to evil present in us all since the fall. Again we return to God's supreme gift, our freedom. Our inner urge to exercise our freedom in choosing evil rather than good is the eternal temptation since the fall. The latter is not history but a parable for all time and true for all humankind; Adam and Eve are all of us. Prayer ensures that we are infinitely more likely to choose the good because it puts us in touch with God the source of all good. With the resultant help of his grace in Christ we can do what even to the godless world seems impossible.

But God, through his Christ and the sacraments and aids of his holy church, can protect and deliver us from the insistent power of the evil one only if we only ask for and avail of his ready at hand helps. Prayer strengthens our will in this regard so that when we face temptation and its vain illusion of happiness, we are more likely to see through and reject it; we are more likely to choose the good we already know by our innermost conscience. Here again prayer perfects the natural law within us, just as the Sermon perfects the inner eye of our mind and soul in relation to seeing and choosing the good.

The final doxology of the Our Father - "for thine is the kingdom, the power and the glory forever and ever, amen" - has not always been added because it is not in the prayer as given by the Lord in scripture. Hence, in Catholicism it was only reinstated after Vatican 11. It was a wise choice. For as I noted above this prayer is about the kingdom come. Maybe the reason why it was dropped was because its association with "power and glory" is the opposite of the beatitudes in many ways, though it refers to God and his transcendent glory and majesty, not man.

But looking at it from another perspective it fits perfectly with all that went before, especially the focus on the Kingdom. That is, man must realize, and this is the Beatitudes in essence, that the kingdoms of this world of which Satan is lord are passing away, illusory, and leave us empty before eternity, but Christ is lord of love, peace, truth, happiness and salvation both for our fullness of joy in this world, and forever and ever, amen.

CHAPTER 29

▼

The 12 Spiritual Paths

The final series of exhortations continue the stress on discipleship as the prerequisite for Kingdom spirituality. All the great injunctions of the Sermon are made possible only in the context of purifying the heart, praying for the right spirit within. Christ not just charts a spiritual morality but also a moral spirituality. Purity of intention and act centered on God and the good of the other are the keys. This is what enables us to exceed the righteousness of the Scribes and the Pharisees. So this is not about religion but pure religion. It's only from a right relationship with the Father, whom we know in secret, that the Sermon's ways to purify the heart, and make us grow in virtue, stem. They are the paths to the Kingdom of the pure heart. They recall all to God's righteousness in the same way as the prophets did, as for example in the words of Joel (2:12-14).

The importance of the paths to holiness, like fasting, is that they are means to purity of heart. They make us part of the Kingdom Christ came to establish and so enable us to inherit its untold blessings. Previous aspects of the Sermon show us what purity of hearts entails, the paths show us how the spiritual basis for that pure heart can be built.

(1) Authentic Fasting

The forty days of Christ's fasting in the desert sets the tone for this means to holiness in the Christian dispensation. It was there in the desert that he purified his heart for his ministry to the world. It was there that his focus became not men's praise or his own wealth and power but total love of the Father and service of humankind; "you shall worship the Lord your God and him only shall you serve". This was later to issue in the church's 40 days of fasting in Lent, a time of returning to the path of righteousness if we've strayed. Fasting is part of a personal and community process of purification, a return to blessedness amid God's people.

There was no extended or formal or required time of fasting in Judaism, nothing like the Islamic Ramadan. But all were encouraged to fast as part of the intensification of prayer and deepening of the spiritual life. Many fasted on Monday and Thursday and during the days of Atonement.

They saw this as a path to holiness of life for it taught humility before God, strengthened prayer and aided alms giving. In Christ's day it had become a way for the religious authorities to show off to win the praise of men.

Jesus asks for the restoration of the real spirit of this practice. Again the heart is the key; it must be orientated towards God and not public show. The latter is no holiness at all, just hypocrisy. It was the custom not to wash or anoint one's face when fasting; the Pharisees used this as a prideful sign to the world that they were fasting. Hence Christ says that one should wash one's face and appear cheerful so no one would know one was fasting except God. The religious authorities fasted from a motive of worldly pride and self-glorification. This was the opposite of the original scriptural motives for fasting, to purify the heart, to renew one's faith and return to right living. Examples of this are the prayer and fasting of the people at Nineveh in a return to God, and David's fasting after his sin in taking his captain's wife by unlawful and corrupt means.

Christ makes it clear to his disciples that he wants a return to the real spirit of fasting. Hence his typical words to disciples in the Sermon are repeated here, "it was said to you in the past but I say to you". The fasting of the disciples should be orientated towards God and come from the heart. So such authentic fasting is related to the central command of the scriptures, loving God with one's whole heart. True fasting says I put God and the kingdom before myself and my satisfactions; I return to righteousness.

Again it is the "more" of Kingdom righteousness, giving all for the sake of the Kingdom, and giving all from the heart as in the beatitudes. Christ says that the only spiritual worth of fasting is if it's done from a heart focused on God. Only as such is it part of our deliverance from evil. It frees us within to do the good deeds that are the Kingdom vocation. There's logic in this, a spiritual logic given in literary language which we might chart as follows:

Chart 11

False fasting

in public to win men's praise result a worldly heart
external righteousness
lack of spirit to do good
treasure on earth

True fasting

in secret focused on God result a pure Godly heart
internal righteousness
internal freedom to do good
treasure stored up in heaven

(2) Building Treasure in Heaven

In this Christ says that true spirituality builds treasure in heaven, as well as making us happy and free within in this world. It frees us from the tyranny of greed and so it makes us happier. If it is orientated towards God it is part of the first great injunction summary of the law: "you shall love the Lord your God with your whole heart and your whole soul and your whole mind". True love of God means loving him more than money or any purely passing worldly goods.

Having treasure in heaven relates to the First Beatitude. Being prepared to sacrifice even worldly gain for God proves that our love is real. It also ensures that we will win a great reward for that love, a reward stored up for us in heaven greater than in any worldly riches. But this too has a reward of happiness in this life. We must not see this in stark dualistic terms. The JBC says that it also refers to things whose fruits we already enjoy in this world while the capital is laid up for us in the life to come, "honoring one's father and mother, deeds of loving kindness, making peace between man and his fellows" (645).

Like the Beatitudes it means happiness and spiritual riches both for this world and the next. There is also a sense of the passing nature of earthly riches and so the foolishness of putting all our trust in them. We should not work just for passing goods; we can't carry riches with us into the grave. This echoes a theme present throughout the psalms, e.g. 49:

> Foolish and stupid perish both alike and
> leave their fortune to others.
> Their tombs are their eternal home,
> their lasting residence, though
> they owned estates that bore their names.
> Do not be afraid when a man grows rich,
> when the glory of his house increases.
> When he dies he can take nothing with him,
> his glory cannot follow him down.

We are to be wise and see that true riches are in God and the service of others. We should amass spiritual riches through personal prayer, fasting, alms giving and authentic communal worship. These are the goods that make us rich in God and increase our union with him. These alone bring lasting riches here and flower at last into eternal glory. By contrast, piling up of material treasures not only does not last, but it makes us uneasy even here for woodworm can destroy our grand houses or robbers break in and steal our gold. Riches can even destroy our souls here and for eternity as Jesus says: "what doth it profit a man if he gains the whole world and suffers the loss of his very soul".

We return to the First Beatitude. Our true happiness here and for eternity is in poverty of spirit. When we are free from the tyranny of possessions we can serve God and others with free hearts and win lasting heavenly riches. The key statement here is that where our treasure is there will our heart be also. If our treasure is in material things we may end up with a material soul for all eternity.

That is, there is a key contrast between the fettered worldly heart and the free God-orientated just heart. The latter radiates goodness and happiness to those around him. We should build in our hearts the treasure we gain from true religious devotion. In today's terms this means practicing true constant prayer, fasting, alms giving, piety, fear of the Lord, faithfulness to the church. Such treasures build up a union with God which swells within us unto eternal life. This is the way to gain the inner "pearl of great price" which is the fruit of prayer. One should sell everything to gain that pearl of spiritual enrichment and peace in Christ and in his worshiping communities today.

(3) Visionary Integrity

The role of godly vision within the Christian communities is often neglected today, but was given central importance in the ancient prophetic tradition. A good example is the text of the prophet Joel, where he prophesies regarding the future Messiah, and the visionary Spirit he will bring both at his coming and at the *Eschaton:*

> I will pour out my spirit on all mankind.
> Your sons and daughters shall prophecy.
> Your old men shall dream dreams,
> And your young men shall see visions (3:1-2).

In the early church the role of tongues and other wonders affirmed the dynamic prophetic aspect of Christian vision. This links with the Sermon injunction that Christians should light up the world. They should not let their light from the Holy Spirit go out or put their inner visionary "lamps" in Christ under a tub.

Here being the "lamp of the body" may also refer to one's role in the Christian community. Each Christian must be a "lamp" for the community. Christ's mention of the "lamp" here has similar connotations to the earlier injunction not to let our "lights" become dim. But here there is a subtle variation. Succumbing to darkness within is given graver connotations. Without the visionary light of God in Christian souls, evil and darkness can return to reign in their hearts, a state even worse than before: "if the light inside you is darkness, what darkness that will be". Again keeping the heart pure and enlightened by Christ in a community of faith and worship is stressed. The equivalent today for Catholics would be attending mass in an active way, nourishing our souls by personal prayer and proclaiming the visions we get from God, for the good of all.

That is, a healthy inner life is achieved through a Christlike church-based spirituality, and to enrich that base some are given special prophetic or visionary roles within the community; like Bernadette of Lourdes or the Fatima seers or Theresa of the Child Jesus in recent times. But all can build the extra light of Christ inside through authentic devout practices. To guard against the pure light of God within turning to darkness, we need constant spiritual nourishment. For the eye mentioned here denotes the inner eye of the soul which must not be obscured by spiritual sloth. We keep the "light inside" bright by building an active spiritual life; this is for our good and that of the church.

This is not inward looking but geared towards mission. As our physical eye illumines the world around us so it must be with the inner eye. So this is a warning not to neglect the practical proclamation of the faith. Great saintly visionaries like Theresa of Avila or John of the Cross were also builders up of the church and founders of religious orders. The Sermon injunction about letting our light shine before men through good works is linked here with keeping the light shining in our own souls first; we can't give what we haven't got ourselves.

I suppose the modern application of this is to keep the light received at baptism burning in our souls by every means of maintaining and furthering our union with God: attending mass; personal prayer at home; reflecting on the Word of God; retreats; contemplative prayer; everyday devotions etc. These necessary nourishments for our souls will enable us to be a light to all around us in our world and will inspire some to become special visionary seers and active missionaries of godly insight to the wider world.

Applying this to modern life, the message is that nourishing our vital "inner man" is always important. One may argue that this is woefully neglected in today's secular materialistic society. All seems surface glitter and superficiality, bombarded as we are by TV ads or vain chat or game shows (George Orwell in his book 1984, saw such distractions as a way the dominant ideology kept the "proles" occupied and so prevented them from questioning the system at any deeper level). Humanity's soul needs nourishment too. We need to keep our inner lights on through soul activities such as fine art, music and literature, and especially through the deep spiritual riches that come only from God. The metaphor Christ uses here is that as a sound eye is the light of the physical body so a sound inner eye in Christ and Kingdom righteousness is the light of the church "body" and the world.

Getting and keeping the heart right and pure in God and before men is the key to happiness. A purely passive personal faith is not enough. Faith is given so that as luminous members of the Kingdom our light and good works can shine before men and glorify our Father in heaven. Like a human father proud of his fine son God will be proud of us as we walk through life lit up by the spiritual grace he provides for us in Christ within his body the Kingdom church, whose great role is to nourish and keep enlightened fully its people's and all humanity's souls, their precious immortal part. If kept at a high spiritual level, they in turn can keep the world's darkness at bay. This in not spiritual narcissism, it is active Christian spirituality and visionary insight leading to healthy active Christian mission to enlighten the world.

(4) Serving God Rather Than Money

A darkness that can dim the individual soul's visionary capacity and indeed the church's mission (with its palaces and so on) is riches. So Christ returns to this theme. Peace and freedom from greed are the two most visited themes in the Sermon because they are related. Hence Christ's strong words here that we cannot be the slave of two masters, of God and money. The humble unassuming service of God and others is like the service of a gentle slave, totally selfless and detached from greedy self-interest. This again recalls the statement that our righteousness must exceed that of the Scribes and Pharisees. They did everything for money, power and glory, oppressing the poor and even representing this as service of God.

This injunction is a warning to the Christian disciples and all people of the world not to make that mistake. Yet the church down the ages consistently succumbed to the temptation to put the power and riches of the institution before the authentic service of the one who had nowhere to lay his head, and who is most present in the poor and vulnerable; hence the seriousness of scandals like child abuse in the church. Love of riches can lead to darkness within. Even recently Pope Francis had to rebuke a bishop who spent 40 million on a lavish extension to a palace for himself. Francis himself lives simply like St. Francis did.

Like St. Paul, Christ goes close to saying that money is the root of all evil and detachment the beginning of all good. This leads on inexorably to the next spiritual path, trust in Providence. What is the antidote to greed? It is serving God and humanity rather than amassing personal wealth. Worldly riches pass quickly to a square box in a few feet of earth.

(5) Trust in providence

At the heart of the Sermon we come a beautiful prose poem of great density and depth; a lyric masterpiece within the Sermon's larger epic. Its primary focus, trust in God's providence, echoes a theme throughout the prophets and especially the psalms, e.g. Ps 114:5-6; 115:10-11. 15-16:

> I trusted, even when I said "I am sorely afflicted";
> When I said in my alarm, "no man can be trusted"

Trust in God rather through every trial and affliction is the characteristic of the just man, the man of steadfast faith. And the psychological and spiritual value of such trust is proved in our age by saints such as Mother Theresa. It enabled her to do great work for the poor despite opposition. Once when some would prevent her from using a disused temple to house the poor saying it would be a desecration she replied that God does not make such distinctions.

Similarly, John Paul 11's motto was Christ's words "do not be afraid for I am with you". It helped him overcome Nazi and communist oppression in Poland, survive the effects of being shot, and make endless travels all over the world even when ill and frail towards the end. Trust in God can be the greatest spiritual dynamic of all in the world.

But Christ is concerned also in this prose poem with trust in God to provide for our material welfare. He has provided enough resources on earth to feed its people well. The UN stated recently that there was enough food on earth to feed 35 times its population. The problem comes from unequal distribution due to human greed. Some in the first world grab too much, so others in the third world have too little. In the beatitudes and here God gives us the remedy, poverty of spirit. The Our Father says to pray and our "daily bread" will be given and Christ says that God understands our physical needs and will provide them if we let him.

So what this tract is mainly concerned with, then, is the undue and enslaving obsession among those who have plenty, with food, clothes and length of life. We hoard money because of a fear of going without it at some stage. So our life is one of continual fear for the future.

Of course we need clothes, food and a good standard of living. That's not what Christ is condemning. The trust of the Sermon elsewhere and the Gospel in general is that all of us should help to bring the basic material necessities to everyone. We should work to eliminate world poverty. It's the undue focus on material things to the destruction of one's soul that Christ is concerned with, a danger to which the rich easily succumb. The verb Christ uses in this respect is "preoccupied" or "absorbed by". If riches have our obsessive attention then we may have no room left for God, others or the things of the soul, like Scrooge. We may lack inner freedom and riches may destroy all that's best in us.

Christ gives beautiful examples of the lilies, birds and grasses which don't have such an obsession yet they are cared for by God. We are more important and should trust that God will care more for us, the glory of his creation, whose souls are eternal; "are you not worth much more than they" (the birds, flowers and grasses God sustains).

Material things will be provided if all share and are happy with enough, so we should focus on the larger things of life, because: "life means more than food and the body more than clothing". Riches alone are not what make people important or better than others. Nor are riches a sign of God's favor, a false Reformation view among some and the genesis of the Protestant ethic. Christ says that this is the worldly view. Our value is in ourselves as God's children; all are his equal children and with our help equally cared for. If we're wise and know that its values within that count, the just values of the Kingdom; if we seek these values first, everything else will follow, especially justice for the earth.

Applying this to today, I suppose one could say that equating our value with riches, the American dream, and saying that otherwise we are "losers" is a fallacy of the world that does not fit well with the Sermon. Moreover, this view that only the rich are "winners" can lead us to despise the poor. Christ criticizes frantic possessiveness, gathering more and more goods, a cult of never enough that is the root of much injustice. The Sermon echoes the parable of the rich man who spent his life filling his barns with goods but of whom Christ says: "fool this night your soul will be required of you, and of what use will your riches be then".

It's in this sense that Christ says to disciples, "oh ye of little faith". It is an admonition, especially to the disciples, against soul-destroying and other-oppressing worldliness. With them, as in the modern obsession with austerity economics, getting and spending can become a fetish, shutting out the light; one is reminded of Wordsworth's lines, "getting and spending we lay waste our powers". The antidote to injustice-promoting materialism Christ provides is trust in providence, concentrating on real just life values.

But he goes further than this by highlighting the uselessness of worry about material things. Such anxiety achieves nothing and can make us careworn and unhappy. Christ's focus is our happiness. Worrying achieves nothing; "can any of you, for all his worrying, add one single cubit to his span of life". So there is a solid logical and psychological truth here that echoes the First Beatitude.

Christ's objective is to free those who have enough, free them from the inner obsession with more and more, so that they may have time for important things in life, nature, beauty, love, God and shaping a just world. There is a lesson there for consumerist society, where many are too busy during the week earning money and at the weekends too busy spending it to have time for visiting sick relatives, going to church, loving their family, culture, recreation etc.

There is no doubt that one can read into this part of the Sermon a strong critique of capitalism, as one can equally read into it a strong critique of communism. Both focus unduly on man's material condition to an unhealthy exclusion of his larger spiritual needs. This leads to an undue narrowing of his horizons and the negation of his transcendent glories and potentialities. The early Christian church was a socialist commune but a larger spiritual perspective underpinned their social practice to ensure all had enough. One can understand then why Pope John Paul 11 criticized the spiritual limitations of both cold capitalism and materialistic socialism in his theological writings.

For there is also a Christian sense in this part of the Sermon of the worldly way as against the Kingdom way, "it is the pagans who set their hearts on these things" (these things being fine clothes, food and riches). Christ does not exclude these things, we should enjoy our life fully, but he points out that our heavenly Father knows we need these things. The question here is one of priority? Christ says "set your hearts on his kingdom first, and on his righteousness and all these other things will be given you as well". The simple word "first" sets the whole debate on a completely different plane.

The focus comes back to the Kingdom as our first priority. It comes back to faith as against lack of it: trust in God as against trust in riches; worldly narrowness as against godly openness; spiritual fullness as against worldly emptiness; mean covetousness as against generous giving; seeking and imitating the giving Kingdom of God as against the enslaving, grasping, avaricious world of the evil one. We are back to the First Beatitude. Christ wants our freedom from useless worry because he loves us.

The paradox is that his is the more successful way in life too. We need a balance of the spiritual and material to reach full human potential. This is proved even in modern life where many financiers and successful business men practice yoga. They empty the mind of clutter and reach for inner peace so as to be successful in business as well as life. The same impulse to peace, away from the clutter and pain of the world, caused the Buddha to seek to rise above life's worries in contemplation. Similarly, Zen Buddhists seek a fuller sense of life and happiness in simple communion with nature. The poems of Basho come to mind.

Christ, the poet is here again asking for purity of heart so that our hearts can be full, poverty of spirit so that we can become rich, meekness so that we can inherit the earth. Even the question of human labor comes into this great Sermon section. Beautiful natural creatures "do not toil nor spin" yet God cares for them. A condemnation of the modern obsession with work, neglecting family or God for ceaseless enslaving money-making is also inferred.

This discourse also questions the obsessive planning ahead which is behind so much frantic accumulation of wealth. Christ says to concentrate on today's problems; "Therefore do not be anxious about tomorrow, for tomorrow will take care of itself. Each day has enough trouble of its own". Again this is the focus of many eastern mystics, liberating concentration on immediate experience.

But Christ takes that further, we have enough to occupy us every day without saddling ourselves with future worries. Not that we shouldn't do some planning ahead, common sense requires that we do so; it is the frantic enslaving obsession with future security that Christ modifies. The concern is with our immediate peace within in God that leads to prosperity in every way for us and the world. The whole section then contains more than the "wisdom of Solomon". Solomon was offered a choice of anything by God, but rather than riches or power he chose wisdom. The same choice is asked of us; we are encouraged to be wise, to be made happy by living the teaching in this central poetic discourse of the Sermon.

(6) Not Judging Anyone

"Judge not - you shall not be judged". Again the eschatological dimension is added by Christ. Those who do not judge others will not be judged by God. Christ is all the time giving a wider heavenly perspective, for a happier life here, a kingdom on earth as well as in heaven: "the amount you measure out is the amount you will be given". The more generous we are the more generous others will be with us. Again the paradox, the more we give the more we will receive. John Paul 11 spent his life going out to others and seven million flocked to Rome for his funeral. Again this teaching is not up in the air.

The beatitude this path links with above all is mercy. If we have true self-knowledge, we see the "plank" in our own eye rather than the "splinter" in our brother's. Self-knowledge then before God means clarity both to see our faults and non-judgmentally to correct those of our brothers and sisters. The parallel in the Gospel is the woman caught in adultery, "let he who is without sin cast the first stone".

Applying this to modern life, I'm shocked by the judgmental lack of mercy in some of the media today. For example, no mercy is shown to those in public life such as priests who fail. They're hounded almost to the grave by a self-righteous fury that's frightening. Recent scandals in the media such as in the BBC show the truth of Christ's words; only he who is without sin should cast stones.

Of course there must be justice for those wronged, this is without question. But harsh punishment must always be tempered by mercy. None of us can afford to be utterly ruthless in our judgments lest we face the wrath of God and man as a result, a point made well in Shakespeare's **Merchant of Venice.** There the young lawyer pleads for mercy from Shylock, who demands his "pound of flesh". So this part of the Sermon has echoes in many human hearts too. Judging the aids victim, or the prostitute, or the failed marriage is not on. We are all sinners, and need the forgiving judgment of God so we should grant a generous measure of the same to others. There is an eschatological warning here. All will face God's final judgment; the judgments we meet out to fellow humans while in this world, Christ says, will determine the judgment we will receive from God at last.

CHAPTER 30

(7) Respecting Sacred Things

"Do not give to dogs that which is holy". Christ articulates here the Old Testament virtue of "fear of the Lord". It is a theme prominent in the history of Israel. We find it in such stories as the destruction of Sennacherib, or the punishments for defiling the Ark of the Covenant, or the "writing on the wall" against the Syrian invader of Israel who used the sacred Temple vessels for pagan orgies. This is true in the modern world also, and has stirred up controversy in relation to blasphemy laws against Islam. New laws have been passed in many countries against stirring up racial and religious hatred.

Even in the modern secular sphere people realize that some things are sacrosanct. The modern fetish for attacking all things holy as some sort of freedom is an example of the opposite. The targeting of faith by cartoonists and media secularists (to reinforce their own irreligious ideology?) is a good example of this; nothing seems beyond the pale. Everything, even the holiest of beliefs, can be thrown before the "dogs".

This is especially true of western secularist attacks on Islam, which is an insult to all the faithful of that creed. Is it really free speech to have the license to insult people's faith with impunity? Ordinary laws condemn malicious slander.

But this aspect of Matthew may refer particularly to the attacks on and persecutions of the early church. Christ is probably referring to the Gospel, in which elsewhere he compares the faith to the "pearl of great price" that we should sell everything to gain. There also he talks about not casting this pearl before swine. So we should not bring sacred things down to the world's crass level. Our Kingdom light mustn't be plunged into darkness and dust.

(8) Believing Prayer

Here Christ returns to the key theme of prayer, hammering the message home, that it is our life. With peace, it is the great theme in the Sermon. Humble prayer is a realization of our need for God and the human fullness found only in him; I recall Jung's view that the death of God is the death of man.

This path echoes the Our Father. Believing prayer sees God as a good Father who always answers our prayers in one way or another. As such it links with trust in God, a powerful theme in the Old Testament, e.g. psalm 69 "answer me, O Lord, for thy steadfast love is good". There is a sense throughout the psalms and prophets that prayer in trouble is always answered by God:

> Lord in trouble I invoke you,
> And you answer my prayer (86:7).

There are clear echoes of this in the Sermon's call for trusting prayer. If we ask or seek or knock it's usually because we are in need of something important, we are in trouble in some way. There is a sense of urgency here and also a surety, as in the psalms, "the door shall be opened to you". It's clear that this is asking God for simple material things also. It suggests the gospel story of the man knocking at his neighbor's door for bread because a friend has come and he has no bread in the house.

Searching, however, suggests more the search for Kingdom truth, "search and you will find". We can only receive the perfect kingdom on earth through our openness to God giving it to us; we can't gain it by our own efforts. But we can get it if we ask humbly for it from God. So the spiritual and eschatological dimensions of trusting prayer are included here. If we knock at heaven's door we will be admitted. Luke adds that especially God will not fail to give the Holy Spirit to those who ask him; all we have to do is open the door of our hearts to his knock. Hence the popular picture, "behold I stand at the door and knock". God can't give us anything, because of our freedom, unless we ask, but when we approach him in humility and trust, recognizing our need, he gives us everything. This confidence that God will answer our prayers is based on his fatherly love and care for us, which is greater than any human father's love; "if you know how to give your children what is good, how much more will your Father in Heaven give good things to those who ask him".

But there is a fine distinction in the phrase "good things". We should ask for "good things", not expect God to answer all our silly petitions, or those contrary to the normal course of nature. Praying to win the Lotto is hardly a guarantee that we will get it. Luke refines this further in saying that God will "give the Spirit" to those who ask. This suggests that it is Christ's Kingdom Spirit that we should ask for most of all, in total trust. This is the spirit of the psalms again, "I trusted even when I said in my alarm no man can be trusted". Humans let us down, but God never does, our prayers are always answered in the best way; this gives us the motivation we need to pray continually, as Paul says, even for the ordinary everyday things we need urgently.

This is not to say that he answers all our prayers. What we ask for may not be good for us, or according to his will, but he always gives "good things" to those who ask. And what we should pray for most of all is for inner strength and faith in the midst of our worst trials and temptations to despair. As the psalms say, even if the sky should fall down, the just man continues to pray to and trust in the Lord. He knows that God will give him the undefeatable and all-transcending Spirit to overcome all things, even intense suffering, and enable him to grow strong thereby in the service of the Lord and all that's good and true and just. The trust that our prayers are invaluable and will always be answered in the best way for us should be the attitude of those who truly belong to the Kingdom.

(9) The Golden Rule.

This is the one element in the Sermon that is not specifically Christian, it was a piece of popular morality common in the Greek and Roman world, "do unto others as you would like them to do unto you". It is close to the Old Testament central rule, love others as you love yourself. But it cannot be put on a par with Christ's weightier and more specifically

Christian demand, "love one another as I have loved you", for this demands total self-giving, a much more serious demand than the golden rule. However, like Christian morality built on the natural law, it was useful for linking his teaching with ground-based morality.

(10) The Two Ways.

Here an antithetical pattern returns that of two opposing ways, the good and the evil or less good one, with a hint again of paradoxical wisdom literature; the narrow way leads to fullness of life. One way leads to life here and hereafter, the other way leads to death here and hereafter. Here we find a series of metaphors about the moral or immoral life. We must choose the narrow gate as against the wide gate, the hard road as against the soft road. This says that true moral living, embodying the Sermon in everyday life, may not be easy but it is more rewarding in the long run. Again there is a sense of "blessed are those who are persecuted in the cause of right", the world prefers those who take its wide godless immoral road, but Christians should be more than worldly wise.

There are hints here also of the gates in Jerusalem; the wide gates were for the rich and the colonists, the narrow gates were for the poor. So this links with "blessed are the poor in spirit". Taking the narrow gate we identify with the poor, we're humble, gentle, meek, merciful, not haughty rulers riding in the wide gate, sure of their power, despising the people. Christ asks us to choose the good way because he knows that because of our free will many choose to go the other way. Indeed he hints that more follow the perverse way of the world rather than God's just way. This echoes his metaphor elsewhere of the primrose path that leads to the everlasting bonfire. As such this spiritual path is a warning to the disciples not to take salvation for granted; they must stay the difficult course.

They must choose the good way and struggle against the opposite which always seems easier. I suppose in that sense, this is the most applied in our world of all the injunctions. So many films and books and plays depict the struggle of good and evil in similar stark terms, such as **The Lord of the Rings** or **Star Wars**. Practically every comic and popular form depicts this struggle as a war of two uncompromising paths, the dark figure of evil and the bright hero of good who always seems to be working against impossible odds but yet wins out in the end. There is a natural popular sense that life is a choice of good or evil paths. There is a struggle between good and evil in the world and our consciences from God tells us to choose the good and just way, no matter how difficult it may seem.

How good and evil is defined, however, is a moot point. In our modern world it has changed hugely. Things like divorce or same sex marriages that would have been seen as totally unacceptable in the past are not seen so by many now. So the gap between our concept of good and our concept of evil is changing. The primrose path is getting wider, conservatives would say, even in popular Christian culture. But certain basic concepts such as willful killing remain, though proportionalism has narrowed basic traditional Christian concepts of evil even further. Yet even when the paths of the world are wider morally, Christ in the form of his Spirit informing legitimate authority in the church says that Christians should still keep to the narrow way, the definitions of good that are rooted in the gospel and the timeless wise traditions of the church. This is a huge challenge, to heed the ageless ways of the church rather than ever shifting worldly values. This leads on to the next path.

(11) True and False Prophecy

The age-old effort by the world to constantly justify evil puts an onus on Christ's disciples to be able to discern true and false prophets. False prophets in the Old Testament told people what they wanted to hear, they justified every evil practiced by those they prophesied to for monetary gain. Though they claimed to speak for God, they really testified against what he wanted. We can understand the rage in the oracles of Jeremiah against false prophets in his day:

> They commit adultery and walk in lies;
> they strengthen the hands of evildoers so that
> no one turns from his wickedness.
> They speak visions from their own minds,
> not from the mouth of the Lord.
> They say continually to those who despise the word of
> the Lord, "it shall be well with you (23:16-18).

Christ compares false prophets to wolves who devour and scatter the flock. Wolves in sheep's clothing, the false prophets preach a disreputable and blasphemous message. There are false prophets today too; how do we know them?

Christ uses a very logical and simple test, their fruits. The good prophets produce good fruits among the flock, the bad the opposite. In the Old Testament, prophets like Jeremiah were persecuted precisely because they wouldn't tell people what they wanted to hear, that their evils were OK. So the true prophet is always prickly, challenging, telling the unwelcome truth no matter what it costs. Incorruptible integrity is their banner and the sense that because they stand for what is good and right and true they stand for God; the true Old Testament prophets say, "it is the Lord who speaks".

Perhaps the true test of the true prophet is paradoxically how much he is persecuted by the world, "blessed are those who are persecuted for the cause of right". As one wise man said the degree to which we are living Christ's truth can be judged by the degree to which we are made to suffer by the contrary world. But there is also the sense of steadfast sticking to the truth here, especially for the early disciples of the Kingdom. They have an infused knowledge of right and wrong from God in Christ through the continuing testimony of the apostles that he taught, and eventually all recognize the truth when it is brought forcefully to their attention; this capacity is there from the conscience and natural law that all share from God. But since the world is imperfect, there is also a tendency in man to falsehood and immorality; and even conscience can be manipulated, made to fit our subjective biases. So there's a warning here for the disciples of keep to the truth they have received from the proper apostolic authorities, to keep to the true way despite persecution. In the church today that still holds true. It's a moral rock of unbroken tradition from apostolic times and the unbroken succession of its authorities, notably the papal succession.

Yet there is a sense also in popular life and culture that the man who stands out because he stands for what is right against the mob is a prophet for his age. Again this is found even in modern life and literature. A modern prophet, for example, may be the man who opposes the ruthless developer whose mine will pollute the environment. The rightness of such prophetic witness is proved by the fact that he and his cause eventually win out, because good people rally round him. The same is true of the man who stands up for oppressed workers, or racially oppressed groups, or poor peasants without a voice. The list is endless of modern prophets. All Christians in the sense of standing for up what is right, are called to be such prophets by their baptism. They are to stand up for God and Christ and all that's good and right and true as mediated by revelation and the church in its unbroken tradition from the apostles, no matter what ridicule they receive from the world. The prophet who is too popular is more likely to be a fraud.

In the Old Testament, the prophet who steadfastly tells the truth often faces not only fierce opposition but even death. Christ is a good example. The last and perfect prophet as the Son of God, he is crucified because of his very innocence, truth and goodness. He felt this rejection when he wept over Jerusalem, like Jeremiah (LK.13:34-35):

> Jerusalem, Jerusalem, you who kill the prophets and stone those who are sent to you! How often have I longed to gather your children, as a hen gathers her brood under her wings, and you refused!

That the true prophet must suffer, was a consolation to the persecuted early disciples, as it is to every true Christian in all ages. That includes prophets and visionaries today. We can know if they are from God by their fruits. I always say to those who ask me if Medjugorje is OK, to look at its fruits. If it is leading to conversion, prayer and healing it is certainly from God; the evil one is hardly going to produce good fruits. We need prophetic visionaries today too and God provides them, Christians called and anointed to be prophets for Christ and the Kingdom at baptism.

CHAPTER 31

▼

Being a True Disciple

This is the last and most important of all the paths. The purpose of the Sermon is to make people faithful followers of Christ and shapers of his just Kingdom. Christ shows us in the paths the inner attitudes that open us to the truth and that empties us and frees us within so that Christ's just Kingdom can make its home in us. So being a true disciple is about the Kingdom come into hearts pure enough for its reception. But this is not just for one's own salvation. It comes in us so that we can be a light of love and goodness to others in active Christian living.

So in this injunction Christ builds another significant wisdom antithesis, between saying and doing; between charismatic self-glorification and active self-giving for God and others. As a witty person put it most Christians instead of following Christ along the way are more often "in the way" or "by the way". Those who cry out to God and prophecy and cast out demons and do miracles in Christ's name may have faith but they will be cast out if they do not practice what they preach; they too may be false self-glorifying prophets. It's listening to Christ's words and acting on them that makes us true disciples.

People who do the will of God won't always be safe from all the storms and attacks from the world, any more than the prophets of old were. But doing God's will is its own reward, and brings life even in the midst of suffering. Again there is a link with the central prayer of the Our Father, "thy will be done on earth as it is in heaven". His teaching is not just words. It is a sure path to happiness here and salvation hereafter if we act on it; if we live it in everyday deeds of kindness and goodness, in striving for what is right even unto intense suffering.

There is another key literary antithesis here, between those who listen to his voice and do his will regardless of what it demands, and those who listen to his voice but don't do his will. Metaphorically, the former build their house on the rock of Christ, the latter on the sands of alternative shifting worldly values.

The powerful metaphoric antithesis here is further extended into the image of the house built on the rock (of Christ) being safe in every storm, and the opposite house built on the sand of false worldly values easily collapsing when buffeted by the storms of life. So there is again a sense here that these injunctions are for our happiness in this world as well, a deeper happiness than the world can give. Only Christ gives an inner spiritual solidity and security to our lives in the midst of life's storms.

All this is also a stern warning to disciples not to build their discipleship on superficial bases of charismatic wonders or showy faith: "It is not those who say to me 'Lord, Lord' who will enter the kingdom of heaven but those who do the will of my Father in heaven"

So the Sermon ends with the simple injunction, that the true disciples of Christ don't just listen to this Sermon, or be drunk with the spirit and indulge in all sorts of self-satisfying wonders, they do what it says in suffering faithfulness and good works. For only living the Sermon makes us safe before the attacks of the evil one and the storms of life. This is the sure house built on the Rock of Christ, the Son of God. Moreover, only living the Sermon will guarantee our eternal salvation; again the eschatological dimension, our future happiness is at stake.

This is a powerful injunction for us today, for the values of the world, or those who appeal to the "spirit" over Christian moral ways as set down by the Church and Peter the rock, should not to distract us from the difficult active moral way of true discipleship. Christ here might be addressing people who say I obey the church, but I obey the "spirit" first. Or those who say I obey my conscience first, which can be just a way of saying I follow my own desires first, my subjective conscience geared to my own easy way, not the harder will of God in self-emptying faithfulness that is yet the true way to happiness.

Pretense and self-deception was the way of the false prophets and disciples. But Christ's is the narrow road that leads to life, the road of self-abasing poverty of spirit, mourning, meekness, mercy, peace, striving and suffering for what is right. It is not the easy worldly or proud self-serving road, but the tortuous path of suffering faithfulness in doing what is right that yet takes us to happiness and glory here and forever in Christ.

This says that the things of the world and its false gods of which Satan is lord - wealth, power, violence, self-glorification and greed, corruption and oppression of others, ignoring of God, pursuit of our ends regardless of who we hurt - seems to satisfy for a while, but are an illusion in the long run, destroying our souls and the world around us, and endangering our immortal souls, even placing us beyond redemption.

Figures in modern literature like Faust or Scrooge or Pincher Martin, or in modern life like Hitler or Stalin, embody this self-destructive illusory way, building their house on the sand of their own passing egotistical desires and worldly values, leaving a trail of human suffering in their wake. Their way leaves them, when sickness or age or death comes, with nothing but emptiness and hatred and alienation from their fellow human beings and God. Some see this as some sort of heroic paganism but it's just stupid self-destruction in body and soul, alienating us from our finer self and from all humane value and sympathy, as well as from the God who created us and loves us and in whom we find our true happiness. That is what the Sermon is really about; the good latent within our human hearts perfected in Christ, flowering into life for us and all those around us, and at last into happiness forever with God our heavenly Father.

Christ in the Sermon is our good Lord. Because he loves us to the point of giving up even his soul at last, he points his Christian disciples towards the narrower but fuller way to life, goodness, peace, truth, compassion, love, happiness and salvation, for their fullness of soul in this world as well as their joyful participation in his Kingdom of heaven on earth, which is also the fuller service of humanity and its justice and peace. And this is also all people's way to lasting joy with Christ and his true disciples and saints in glorious light forever and ever, amen.

CHAPTER 32

Is the Sermon Excessive Idealism?

Some raise the question of the practicality of this moral code? Davies notes that many dismiss it as too idealistic. But great thinkers such as Tolstoy or Gandhi or John Paul 11 didn't think so. It is only if we view it in terms of what one can achieve by oneself that it seems idealistic. But this ignores the role of grace, the infinite power of the Risen Lord among us. Indeed, it's in this surpassing of what is possible by people alone that the Sermon situates what's challenging and specific in Christian morality. Harrington sums up this in the concept of "the more" which goes beyond normal concepts of the "law" to higher aims, to striving for "the maximum...possible"(81).

For example, Christ says to love one another as "he loved us". This means total self-giving, even of one's life, even for a "bad person". That is what Christ asks, however more worldly moralists might frown. To the worldly wise, a morality won at the cost of intense personal humiliation is foolishness. Yet this is true morality; for it's based on a steadfast decision of will, and the immense freedom to do what is right for God and others regardless of the cost to oneself. If one weighs the cost one is already diffusing the challenge, accepting the mediocre. In this morality we never say "now I have done all the law requires, now I have done enough". Harrington elaborates:

> To understand this idealism, it may be helpful to distinguish between two different kinds of moral demand. Some moral demands are to be observed perfectly right away, for instance, that we should not injure another. But in the case of the other kind of demand, we will spend a lifetime responding ever more perfectly, for instance demands of integrity or of enemy love. The idealism of Jesus refers to the latter. But his emphasis is not so much on the gradualness of the achievement as on treating the ideal as serious and urgent (82).

If societies change, if they become more permissive, are Christians to follow the way of the man on the Clapham bus? The bar must be set high, so that we have something to aim at, something challenging to stimulate our souls into greatness. For if morality is just what everyone can easily achieve, we will have no saints, those who are recognized as the pinnacles of every culture. Christ sets the bar high to challenge us to heroic holiness and thousands, indeed billions, if we include all the secret saints down the ages, have shown that this is eminently possible. One might even say that by God's grace in Christ we can do almost anything to fulfill our dreams and he came, as he says, that we may have life and have it to the full.

We find this striving for perfection in all cultures worthy of the name, from the Islamic Sufis to Hindu holy men and women that all revere. That all cannot achieve it, does not compromise the importance of the ideal as something for everyone to aim in the various degrees of which they are capable. I am reminded of the story of a man visiting a monastery. Thousands of monks bustled around at various tasks. The man asked the abbot: "how many disciples do you have here, holy man". "Oh one or two", he replied.

Any claim that one cannot live Christ's master way leaves out the role of grace. All can follow him in various degrees and aim as high as they can but they need the challenge. It's in this greater challenge that the Sermon is based on, yet way beyond, the Commandments. It's a more positive, interior, and fulfilling expansion of the Ten Commandments, so as to constitute a true moral "theology". Way beyond the minimum legal standards of behavior that some in the past and some in modern society see as moral living, it proposes attitudes and dispositions that if implemented would lead to the kingdom of God, man's final happiness and perfection, and a perfect world, the Kingdom of heaven brought to earth. It would bring a just society and make us all blessed. And surely that is what everyone wants, the morality not of what is but what all good men wish would be, the shining world we all want in our hearts.

So far from being a restricting law it is a recipe for true happiness, freedom, peace and glory both for here and hereafter. It would shower on us God's abundant blessings, salvation at all levels, even that of nature, beyond compromises and greedy short cuts. Some, like the exponents of more pragmatic moral codes, may make compromises with the world, but the true home of the true prophet is the radical way of Christ. Listening to the radio the other day I heard a spokesman for the White House responding to the death of hundreds of innocent people in an allied bombing somewhere. He called it "a proportional response". Does anything in fact justify the killing of hundreds of innocent civilians? What about not returning evil for evil?

The sign of real Christian morality is if the Sermon is really alive among us in true peace, joy, humility, gentleness, mercy, and a final fulfilling of our frail thirst for Righteousness? It's no use keeping the letter of the law if we don't have humility, love, mercy, purity, peace and goodness in our hearts. And because we are limited that can only be achieved by the miracle of the kingdom; the new overflowing grace of Christ, the guidance of the gospel and the support of his holy community as a vital conduit of grace and Christ's all-encompassing spiritual presence.

For the Sermon is really about imitation of him, not slavish imitation, but imitation of his filial relationship with God. So at the sermon's core is the Our Father. It says everything. With God as father, through the redeeming action of Christ, we are a new humanity that gives God glory by doing more than what was humanely possible by fallen man. Christianity is "Thy Kingdom come". As John Paul 11 notes:

> The Christian, thanks to God's revelation and to faith, is aware of the "newness" which characterizes the morality of his actions; these actions are called to show the dignity and vocation bestowed on him by grace" (111).

Such morality is known in an integral way by God's supernatural revelation and it's living out in Christ's new Kingdom community, for we need such community support, we can't do everything it requires on our own.

What Christ offers is a perfect Kingdom way, divine laws which serve God and humankind. Doing God's will in "its entirety" is hallowing his name; creating a "heaven" on earth; ensuring that ultimate justice is done on earth; making sure that all get their "daily bread" (materially through good standards of living and spiritually through the Word and Eucharist); ensuring that all have access to God's "forgiveness" and reflect it to others; ensuring that all are "delivered from evil", the aim of all morality.

This is not something we can achieve by ourselves alone, for within, as Paul says, is another law of sin and death; but in union with God in Christ within a sacramental community of faith it is more than possible. It is made possible through that community's spiritual guidance and support; through true prayer of the heart, fasting and alms giving; through laying up treasures in heaven, serving God rather than just money or perishable earthly goods; through trusting in Providence and so on. In these ways the Sermon lays a foundation in humankind of a spirituality that makes all morality possible and lasting. This sure house is built on Christ's great rock of truth if we enter in at the narrow gate; avoid self-righteous morality fixed on our own self-importance and are a true rather than a false prophet.

The latter offers the easy way, Christ gives difficult freeing ideals. Become interior righteousness by prayer, fasting and active charity, such good actions identify the truly moral man; "by their fruits you will know them". The Pharisees produced no such fruit; the interior ground out of which it might grow was barren. Only from Christ's pure ground in his holy church can such fruits naturally spring.

Only from the Sermon's pure spiritual ground we can attain the fullness of the Kingdom of Heaven on earth. A sure way to build that Kingdom is through its central virtues: poverty of spirit, meekness, mourning, compassion; striving for what's right and facing opposition as a result; having peace within and living justly and peacefully in harmony with ourselves, others, the world, nature, and God; living a life of faithful, true and enduring love in our relations with the opposite sex and our soul mate chosen by God; having generous hearts to always go the extra mile in our love of God and others; growing through prayer and the Eucharist in a deep relationship with the living God, our Father in heaven; in Christ's power as Risen Lord overcoming evil; forgiving freely; growing within through prayer, fasting and alms giving so we can be a light of glowing goodness to the world; being faithful disciples of Christ and so striving to be perfect as our heavenly Father is perfect.

I say "striving" for none of us will ever be perfect, that is for the angels; holiness is in the struggle. It's as Von Balthasar says letting the light of the prototype fall on the image, giving at least our frail humanity the capacity to attain to its full final dignity and truth (283). It's as far as possible with the help of grace aiming to attain the perfect way to a happy life here and hereafter. And in the process helping to reshape the world into the glorious innocent creation it was at the beginning. This is idealistic but it can be reached to a greater or lesser extent as has been attested to by millions of saints in the church visible and invisible; for it's being immersed in Jesus Christ and his values, and he is Lord of love, truth, beauty, happiness and salvation both for this world and forever and ever, amen.

CHAPTER 33

Conclusion

The content of the Sermon is so beautiful and pure it begs the question as to how we might live it today? We have tried Communism, Fascism, Maoism and all sorts of short-sighted human systems, why not Christ's master plan for humanity? Its viability has been proved by canonized saints and secret saints everywhere. It has produce luminous holiness - from St. Francis, poor in spirit, to Mother Theresa helping the poor beyond the call of duty. It is universal. It gels with those of other religions who seek the perfect path. The quest for a pure heart and integral living is a universal ideal seen in holy men and women of various cultures and civilizations. Humanity has ever quested for spiritual and moral wholeness and a just world. This is seen in the modern exemplars of the Sermon's values in both the secular, religious and social area such as Mandela, Gandhi, Luther King or John Paul 11.

The Sermon resonates with truth, especially when the beatitudes are expanded to eight in Matthew five to seven.

Though some scholars say this was a later collection of Christ's saying with Keryma additions, this view has been refuted by others. Most now see it as an authentic entity from Christ as in the recent internet commentary on of the Sermon by Arthur. It is Matthew's foundational account of Christ's early preaching (e.g. the "two Gospel" theory of Griestbach puts Matthew as the original gospel, and there is much to commend this view, not least that it was the view in the early church). The fact that James, writing soon after the resurrection, echoes the Sermon, often quoting it word for word, and encapsulating its spirit in his epistle, proves this. Moreover, Christ's whole approach in the Gospels is similar to the whole trust of the Sermon. Throughout the gospel we see similar prophetic attacks on the Pharisees and their morality as rigid law, and consistent radical demand for a newer fuller discipleship. There is a consistent call to establish and make possible a new Kingdom of God on earth such as the Sermon articulates. That's why he proclaimed the latter at the beginning of his public ministry, at the same time as he proclaimed the coming of the Kingdom in his person.

In any case can we really distinguish between the Christ of the Keryma and the historical Christ? Of course not, for what the Gospels are is a deeper biography of Christ, a deeper understanding of his reality under the power of his Spirit sent to the early church; for Christ says that when the Spirit comes "you will understand all things".

Moreover, the Sermon is Christ. Its declarations of various forms of "blessedness" show God dwelling with his people as the Christ, who outlines all that's good for us, invites us to a blessed way, and gives us new imperatives to do good and avoid evil for our happiness in this world as much as the next. Thereby we save our world too.

LEARN FROM ME: AN EXPOSITION OF THE SERMON

What we see in the Sermon as a whole is a complete moral way that could only have come from God, for it embodies the pure innocent faithful heart of God and his loving perfect plan for human happiness. This is the final covenant written on the heart which Jeremiah proclaimed, and which is associated with the coming of the Messiah:

> Deep within them I will plant my law, writing it on their hearts. Then I will be their God and they shall be my people (31:33-35).

We find the same in Ezekiel, where he says that God will remove our hearts of stone and give us hearts of flesh instead (11:19-20). In the same way the Sermon sets two things in opposition, the "hardness of heart" of those who rely on law yet fails to care for God or others, and the heart of flesh, the gentle heart of the new disciple of Christ. The latter's model is the Lord himself: "learn from me because I am meek and humble in heart and you will find rest for your souls". The purpose of the Sermon then is imitation of Christ's purity, innocence and gentleness of heart. The image of the Sacred Heart is also the image of the Sermon.

In that it is not a burden but a true liberation, a blessed way. Hence Christ's added words in relation to following himself: "for my yolk is easy and my burden light". This is not to shackle us but to free us, not to curtail our freedom but to enable it, not to curtail our enjoyment of life but to make it more complete: "I came that you may have life have it to the full". The hard heart, the possessive heart, the unmerciful heart, the warring and vengeful heart, the narrowly loving heart brings no inner or enduring happiness to its possessor, such as the heart of love that is Christ does.

The central antithesis in the Sermon then is between hardness of heart as against softness of heart, or the closed heart as against the open heart. This is what we find also in all the prophets, the hard closed nature of Israel to their message from God, as the psalms say: "oh that today you would listen to his voice, harden not your heart". This open heart of love is the key to the Sermon. For we cannot build the perfect kingdom of God in Christ on our own, we can only have hearts open for its reception as God offers it to us on the cross. But Christians dare not reject it lest we renew the anguish Christ felt at his rejection by his own:

> Jerusalem, Jerusalem, you that kill the prophets and stone those who are sent to you! How often have I longed to gather your children, as a hen gathers her chicks under her wings, and you refused! (Lk13:34-35).

Whether the values of the Kingdom come or not is our choice rather than God's. But the Sermon shows the way for the wise to follow. It is both a real way to individual perfection, and the way for all to achieve a truly just world. Hence the French and American Revolutions, with their cries of liberty, fraternity, and equality are partly in its spirit. So are the best socialist ideals. But in contrast to them it says that a fully just world can't be imposed by force; it can only come about by each individual having a change of heart. French terror and Marxist totalitarianism prove the uselessness of the way of force to achieve the just world. It's a peaceful revolution within that Christ asks for. For the human heart can't be compelled, it can only open up to receive and do the truth freely. That's what the Sermon asks.

For it's about being happy and free, open hearted children of God and treating others as his children and our brothers and sisters in Christ. It's about turning a fallen and broken world into Christ's just and loving kingdom. It's about having all we need and ensuring that others have what they need, spiritually and materially. It's about accepting the Father's healing forgiveness. It's about being delivered from the power of evil. It's about abhorring terrible totalitarian repression and war. It's about realizing that we cannot save ourselves. It's about accepting our heavenly Father's deliverance freely, for he cannot force us. It's about being his self-effacing love to the world. It's about serving our present and ultimate immortality, Christ's benevolent wish to free the world from death. It's about being the gentle Christ to all who mourn. It's about being Christ on the cross begging all to choose his gentle way. It's about glory, peace, joy and rest for our souls. It's about overflowing life and peace for the world. It's being perfect as our heavenly Father is perfect.

It isn't slavish imitation. No one can be perfect, for we are but flesh. It's keeping up the struggle to be as good as we can be. For even the saints were not flawless paragons. We get up again and again when we fall, tend to rather than ever achieve the moral purity of God. Even the saints constantly complained about their sins. In filial relationship with God, they were conscious of how imperfect they were. Yet at the Sermon's core is the struggle to be like our good Father, giving him glory by doing everything as far as possible in his image: "let your light shine before men so that seeing your good works they may give glory to your Father in heaven". So it's about living our faith in charitable action.

It's about the coming of the Messianic Kingdom dreamed of by the prophets. It's the restoration of the innocence of the original creation. We renew the face of the earth through the means Christ outlines and makes possible by his grace. So that it will be complete when he comes to present the Kingdom to the Father at the end of time, a completion prefigured at his resurrection. Living the Sermon will ensures that we will go out to meet him then with all the saints in the final heavenly Kingdom. In the meantime we serve the Kingdom by God's grace, the Word, and the Eucharistic power of the risen Christ present in the church.

Christ handed over the Kingdom to us in trust. We dare not let him down; for there is the other possibility that Christ mentions: "When the Son of man comes will he find any faith on earth". So in prayer like the Our Father we pray constantly for the full coming of this Kingdom, for our and humanity's sake.

Each person's perfecting in Christ is also the perfecting of humanity. Again one might think of this as too idealistic but, as mentioned, it is a search found in every culture, from Buddhist to Hindu monks to Islamic Sufis to Christian contemplative and active religious. All people potentially seek greatness and glory in being part of something greater than us, humanity's perfection.

By situating prayer at the Sermon's center, Christ affirms its huge role in bringing about the perfection outlined in the Sermon. Through prayer we address the Father, hallow his name, further union with him, and ensure that by his grace all will follow his way to full life here and hereafter.

So returning to the question of the Sermon's viability, the answer is that it's not something we can achieve by ourselves. In that sense the exhortations are both too idealistic and not idealistic at all. It's like the marriage ideal, people say it's so difficult to live but here the church ceremony and the sacramental grace that it gives is ignored. God's powerful

Grace in Christ enables us to do what seems impossible to a more unredeemed cynical world.

Here Christ addresses the perennial heresies of Christians and of the world, that we can be our own Savior or that we do not need to be saved at all. All the godless utopian systems that caused so much havoc in our age were rooted in such heresy, our arrogance and lack of humble recognition of our need for God's redeeming presence in our lives, the original arrogance of Satan. For as Paul says, there is always another law of sin and death within us that only God can heal. In union with God in Christ as supreme Savior we can each in our own way achieve the perfect good presented to us in the Sermon. The means for its fulfillment are given within the Kingdom community of faith, worship, living truth and charity which is the people of God. This is the visible church. But it also has an invisible and wider universal mystical aspect, the church of all good people saved in Christ and inspired by his living Spirit. The visible and invisible church is everywhere, forever, and is the all-powerful and perfect restorer of humankind.

SELECT BIBLIOGRAPHY

The Catechism of the Catholic Church (Dublin: Veritas, 1994) referred to as "the Catechism".

Bligh, John. The Sermon on the Mount: a Discussion on Mt 5-7 (Slough: St. Paul Publications, 1975).

Davies, W.D. The Setting of the Sermon on the Mount (Cambridge University Press, 1964).

Fuellenbach, John. The Kingdom of God (New York, Orbis Books, 1995).

Harrington, Donal. What is Morality? (Dublin: The Columba Press, 1996).

Hendrickx, Herman. Sermon on the Mount (Manila: East Asian Pastoral Institute, 1979).

John Paul 11. Veritatis Splendor (London: Catholic Truth Society, 1993).

Ed. Charles E.Curran and Richard A.McCormack, S.J. John Paul 11 and Moral Theology (New York, Paulist Press, 1998).

John P. Meier. Matthew (Dublin: Veritas, 1984).

Schnackenburg, Rudolf. All Things are Possible to Believers: Reflections on the Lord's Prayer and on the Sermon on the Mount (Westminister: John Knox Press, 1951).

Stott, John. Christian Counterculture: the Message of the Sermon on the Mount (London: Intervarsity Press, 1978).

Tugwell, Simon O.P. Reflections on the Beatitudes (London: Longman, 1979).

Von Balthasar, Hans Urs. "God is his Own Exegete", from Communio, winter 1986, pp. 280-7.
Love Alone: the Way of Revelation (London: Sheed and Ward, 1992).

Ed. Raymond E. Brown, S.S., Joseph A. Fitzmeyer, S.J., Roland A. Murphy, O.Carm. The New Jerome Biblical Commentary (London: Goeffrey Chapman, 1997). Referred to as JBC.

More Books

I want morebooks!

Buy your books fast and straightforward online - at one of the world's fastest growing online book stores! Environmentally sound due to Print-on -Demand technologies.

Buy your books online at
www.get-morebooks.com

Kaufen Sie Ihre Bucher schnell und unkompliziert online - auf einer der am schnellsten wachsenden Buchhandelsplattformen weltweit!

Dank Print-On-Demand umwelt-und ressourcenschonend produziert.

Bucher schneller online kaufen
www.morebooks.de

OmniScriptum Marketing DEU GmbH
Bahnhofstr. 28
D- 66111 Saarbrucken   info(i,,omn1scriptum.com
Telefax: +49681 9381 567-9   www.omn isrn ptum.com

www.ingramcontent.com/pod-product-compliance
Lightning Source LLC
Chambersburg PA
CBHW071430070526
44578CB00001B/56